D0007983

6. Australia 7. Austria 8. Baham... ...Belgium

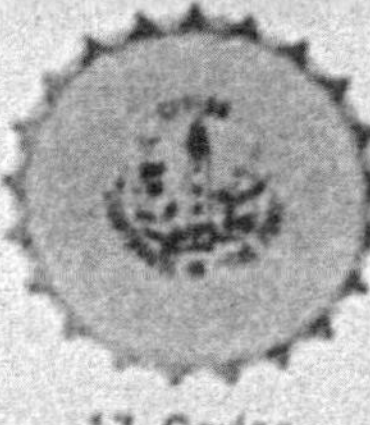

16. Canada 17. Ceylon 18. Chile 19. Colombia 20. Republic of the Co...

...Dominican Republic 27. Ecuador 28. Egypt 29. El Salvador 30. Ethiopia

36. Ghana 37. Gibraltar 38. Grenada 39. Guadeloupe 40. Guam

46. Iceland 47. India 48. Indonesia 49. Iran 50. Iraq

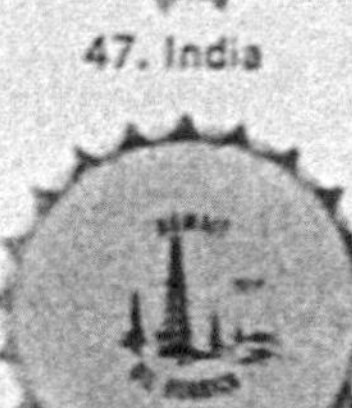

56. Kenya 57. Kuwait 58. Lebanon 59. Liberia 60. Malagas...

2. Aden
3. Angola
4. Antigua
5. Argentina
Bermuda
12. Bolivia
13. Brazil
14. British Guiana
Costa Rica
22. Cyprus
23. Dahomey
24. Denmark
Finland
32. Formosa
33. France
34. French Guiana
35. Germany
Guatemala
42. Haiti
43. Holland
44. Honduras
Ireland
52. Italy
53. Ivory Coast
54. Jamaica
55. Japan

COCA-COLA SUPERSTAR

FIORA STEINBACH PALAZZINI

New York • London • Toronto • Sydney

The publishers of this English edition wish to thank The Coca-Cola Company, Atlanta, Georgia, for all their help with the preparation of this book. Mr. Philip F. Mooney, Manager, Archives Dept., was particularly helpful in clarifying a number of historical points and supplying pictures. Bruce Gilbert and Michael Ellison also assisted with advice as the project proceeded.

First edition for the United States and Canada published in 1989 by Barron's Educational Series, Inc. in association with David Bateman Ltd., "Golden Heights," 32–34 View Road, Glenfield, Auckland 10, NEW ZEALAND

Original edition © Idealibri, via S. Tomaso 10, Milano, first published 1986.

English edition © 1988 David Bateman Ltd.

All rights reserved. No part of this book may be reproduced in any form by photostat, microfilm, xerography, or any other means, or incorporated into any information retrieval system, electronic or mechanical, without the written permission of the copyright owner.

All inquiries should be addressed to:
Barron's Educational Series, Inc.
250 Wireless Boulevard
Hauppauge, New York 11788

Coca-Cola, Coke, Diet Coke, Cherry Coke, Fanta, Sprite are registered trademarks of The Coca-Cola Company. Except where otherwise credited, illustrations reproduced in this volume are the exclusive property of The Coca-Cola Company.

International Standard Book No. 0-8120-5998-0
Library of Congress Catalog Card No. 88-23585

Library of Congress Cataloging-in-Publication Data
Steinbach Palazzini, Fiora
Coca-Cola superstar / Fiora Steinbach Palazzini/
p. cm.
Translated from the Italian.
ISBN 0-8120-5998-0
1. Coca-Cola Company — History.
2. Soft drink industry — History
I. Title
HD9349.S634C68 1989
338.7'66362'0973—dc19

88-23585
CIP

Printed in Hong Kong by Everbest Printing Co., Ltd

CONTENTS

Chapter 1

ORIGINS

It all started in the back of a modest drugstore in Atlanta . . . or more accurately in Knoxville, Georgia, USA, where, in 1833, John S. Pemberton, the genial inventor of Coca-Cola, was born.

Abraham Lincoln was just 24 years old and Napoleon Bonaparte had been dead for only 12 years. Colt had not yet invented the revolver, nor had Morse invented the telegraph or Freud been born. But a new world, rich in promises and scientific progress, was about to start. Pemberton, as a boy, showed such great curiosity and interest in research and scientific subjects that his teachers convinced his parents to send him to study chemistry at a college in

Macon. Later, with a certificate in his pocket, many ideas in his head, and young wife at his side, 23-year-old Pemberton went south to Columbus to open a shop of his own where he could experiment and sell his products.

But he had not bargained with history.

On April 4, 1861 President Lincoln made the famous speech that in one blow swept away many illusions. The American Civil War had begun. Pemberton, like so many others, was swept into the fighting and fought bravely at the head of a cavalry battalion. But his predominant thought and hope was to return to a quiet and industrious life, devoted to research, trading, and his family.

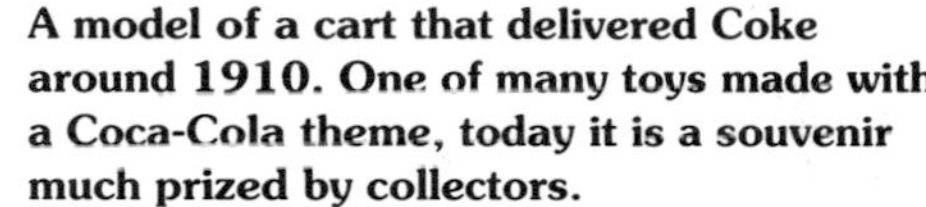

A model of a cart that delivered Coke around 1910. One of many toys made with a Coca-Cola theme, today it is a souvenir much prized by collectors.

8

THE INVENTION OF COCA-COLA

When the war ended, many people felt as if not 4 but 40 years had passed. The South was a desolate scene of misery and death, and Lincoln was murdered by a fanatical madman before he could start reconstruction work.

Things were difficult and bitter: the inhabitants of the southern states, defeated but not beaten, had to roll up their sleeves and start work again . . . just like Scarlet O'Hara in *Gone With the Wind*. John Pemberton found himself with nothing, and decided, with his wife, to try his fortune in Atlanta, where he soon managed to establish himself as a wholesale pharmacist. At first he was only moderately successful, but he persevered with his chemical formulas and sales of his products — remedies for all ills, from baldness to coughs — gradually grew. But still he was not satisfied. His secret ambition was to create a truly original product, one that would bring recognition of his talent, more so than his Indian Queen Hair Dye, Triplex Liver Pills, or Globe of Flower Cough Syrup . . .

Above: The Atlanta drugstore where Pemberton first produced and sold the secret-formula syrup.
Opposite: John Pemberton, pharmacist and the father of Coca-Cola.

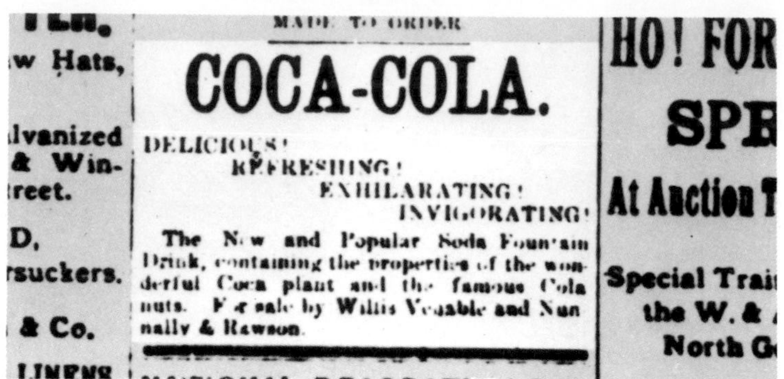

MADE TO ORDER

COCA-COLA.

DELICIOUS!
REFRESHING!
EXHILARATING!
INVIGORATING!

The New and Popular Soda Fountain Drink, containing the properties of the wonderful Coca plant and the famous Cola nuts. For sale by Willis Venable and Nunnally & Rawson.

The first-ever advertisement for Coca-Cola —
Atlanta Journal, **May 29, 1886.**

AND SO COCA-COLA WAS BORN

When did the idea that led to the creation of the drink symbol of modern times, Coca-Cola, first enter John Pemberton's mind?

In 1885 the pharmacist produced a tonic, French Wine Coca, rather similar to Coca-Cola. Later Pemberton modified the formula by omitting the alcohol and adding other vegetable essences. The new syrup, still without a name, was meant to be a quick remedy for headaches! And here the legend begins. The story goes that Pemberton discovered some of the shop boys (another version says two of his friends) were diluting the new syrup with water and drinking it to quench their thirst in the hot summer weather. He tasted it himself, and discovered that the syrup, further diluted with club soda, was pleasant and refreshing to drink. Thus Coca-Cola was born.

The legend continues that he first produced the syrup in a three-legged bran pot in his backyard. He then carried a jug of it down the street to Jacobs' Pharmacy where, on Saturday May 8, 1886 it was sold for the first time, at five cents a glass. That same year, in New York, the Statue of Liberty was unveiled. Both the statue and the drink were destined to become legendary symbols of the new America.

And the name? One of Pemberton's partners, Frank Robinson, suggested Coca-Cola Syrup and Extract, which John Pemberton was quick to shorten to Coca-Cola.

The name certainly contributed to its popularity: four syllables, almost without a nationality, understandable and easy to pronounce in most languages all around the world.

Coca-Cola's early development continued in a casual fashion. For instance, its trademark was stumbled on accidentally. Pemberton wanted something really original, but could not find it. Then, one day when opening the account book in which his partner, Robinson, diligently recorded the business of the pharmacy, he realized the trademark was there before his eyes — the script used by Robinson resulted in the name Coca-Cola being written in a flourishing yet simple style that had immediate impact. He decided to use it. Later, in 1893 it was registered and today is recognized world-wide.

On May 29, 1886 Coca-Cola was advertised for the first time in the Atlanta daily — "Coca-Cola, Delicious! Refreshing! Exhilarating!" The drink was ready . . . but the public was not quite.

A syrup urn used as a premium in the 1890s and now very valuable.

ALMOST A FAILURE

In most legends the hero must overcome many obstacles to reach his goal. So it was for Coca-Cola. Despite the enthusiasm of a small group of devoted consumers, it did not achieve a major breakthrough to the public in its early days. During the first year only 25 gallons of syrup were sold, corresponding to 13 glasses per day. At 5 cents per glass it didn't produce much revenue! It was almost a disaster, as Pemberton had spent more on advertising than he had earned. To avoid ruin, Pemberton, by now 56 years old and in failing health, gradually sold parts of his business to various partners. Just before his death in 1888 he sold his remaining interest in Coca-Cola to Asa G. Candler, then the only one to understand the drink and perceive its enormous potential. A young and ambitious Atlanta merchant, on Pemberton's death he became the sole owner of Coca-Cola. Nothing was left to the pharmacist's heirs, probably because Pemberton had not really believed Coca-Cola could become a success. As sometimes happens to great talents, Luck had kissed him on the forehead, but he had not recognized it. It is said that Lady Luck is blind — she certainly didn't see Pemberton.

$1200 FOR AN EMPIRE

Candler, on the contrary, could see the way clearly. He bought all the equipment and machinery to manufacture the drink, and its formula — which Pemberton had kept a strict secret — for just $1200. It was the best spent money of his whole life.

Asa G. Candler came from an old Anglo-Saxon family that had emigrated to America in 1700. He would never have become the shaper of Coca-Cola's fortune (and his own) had it not been for the Civil War. The well-to-do Candlers had decided that their intelligent son should become a doctor, but fate upset their plans. After the war, they found themselves dispossessed of all property and goods, and for young Asa there was nothing else to do but to abandon his studies and seek his fortune in Atlanta. Like many self-made men, Asa Candler began with little money to his name — according to his biographers, exactly $1.75.

He tried trading and soon realized he had a certain talent for business. He always followed his instincts, even when buying Coca-Cola, for then it was practically bankrupt. In 1890 he abandoned all his other interests, which included dealing in perfumes and toothpastes and devoted himself body and soul to the development of Coca-Cola. On January 29, 1892, with his brother and a couple of friends, he founded the Coca-Cola Company, an organization that still exists.

Asa G. Candler, who turned Pemberton's syrup into an industry.

A STAR IS BORN

Merit must be given to Pemberton for inventing the perfect mixture of ingredients that gives Coca-Cola its unique bouquet, unchanged since then. But Candler must be given all the credit for believing in the product to the point of spreading it through the whole country without being daunted by the initial failures. And soon he was rewarded. Business flourished year by year, so much that by 1895 he had offices in Dallas, Chicago, Los Angeles and, soon after, in Philadelphia. Coca-Cola, at the end of the century, was already the best-known drink in the United States. In 1896 Candler was able to announce that for the first time the drink had crossed the border to begin spreading triumphantly through Canada, Hawaii

1891: the first Coca-Cola calendar. Candler's name appears, but the logo is different from the now familiar one which is protected by copyright throughout the world.

and Mexico. From the 25 gallons sold by Pemberton in 1886, it had progressed to 281,055 gallons in 1899, then to 6,767,822 in 1913 . . . and so forth.

By 1916, when Candler retired as President of the company at the age of 65, Coca-Cola had become one of the country's great commercial successes.

When Candler died in 1929, Atlanta declared a day of public mourning. Squares, streets, parks, hotels were dedicated to his name and southern men gave tribute to one of their number who had contributed so much to the development and wealth of Georgia.

LUCK IN A BOTTLE

To the early pioneers of Coca-Cola, Pemberton, Robinson and Candler, should be added the name of the first Coca-Cola bottler, Joseph A. Biedenharn, a merchant from the little town of Vicksburg on the banks of the Mississippi.

He had been looking for a way to serve the drink at a picnic. The syrup was shipped from Atlanta in red barrels, and then had to be mixed in a glass with club soda, which was not very convenient. He used a bottle called a Hutchinson, which was available for any type of drink at the time. It had the same capacity as the contemporary bottles and the name of his company was inscribed on it. There is one at the Coca-Cola Museum in Atlanta.

Satisfied by his innovation, the young merchant sent a dozen of them to Candler, who answered politely but without enthusiasm. Strangely, the great president of Coca-Cola did not understand, either then or later, the importance of this innovation, which could have multiplied the size of his business. And Biedenharn made no attempt to market his bottled Coca-Cola outside the state of Mississippi, while Candler continued to focus his advertising and promotion on developing soda fountain sales.

A DOLLAR FOR AN EMPIRE

But the future of Coca-Cola was in the bottle. Perhaps Candler belonged by then to another generation of men who had fought and built, risked and gained, but were unable to look to the future, to the new century, to widening frontiers. Others, however, were ready; and

Top left: Joseph A. Biedenharn, the first bottler in Vicksburg, Mississippi. Right: Benjamin F. Thomas; and (lower left) Joseph B. Whitehead, two friends from Chattanooga who obtained the US bottling concession from Candle. Opposite: Atlanta's Coca-Cola Bottling Company, opened in 1900.

they came on the scene at the right time, with the right ideas, and so shared in much of the wealth and glory resulting from the triumphant advance of the drink. They were two young, enterprising attorneys, also from the South: Benjamin F. Thomas, from a modest family, but very intelligent and ambitious; and Joseph B. Whitehead, more worldly, and decisive and able. They were both from Chattanooga, Tennessee.

How did it happen that the two young attorneys, together opted for Coca-Cola rather than the law? The story goes that Thomas owed his flash of inspiration to the time he spent in Cuba, during the short clash with Spain in 1898. Having no alcohol to drink he discovered

solace in bottles of a local fizzy beverage, possibly pineapple flavored. He was so enthusiastic that he talked about it back home. Whitehead suggested he try, as a substitute, Coca-Cola, then still sold exclusively as a syrup mixed with club soda in a soda fountain. Thomas liked it, and the pair quickly hit upon the idea of commercially bottling Coca-Cola.

After long discussions, they decided to try to meet with Candler. They were helped by a mutual acquaintance, and the meeting was fixed for a day in June, 1899. Imagine the trepidation of the two when they met the president, a rich, successful, mature man who was not known for being excessively sociable. They pleaded their cause, asking for a bottling contract not only for one state but for the whole country. Candler thought about it, but not for long. The contract was signed, much, much more easily than the two young men could have imagined . . . and the cost of the transaction was one dollar! Yes, for one dollar (that he never cashed) Candler surrendered the right to bottle Coca-Cola in almost the entire United States.

Candler did not grasp the importance of the operation, but who else, in his place, would have understood it? As one writer put it, "At that time, only a visionary or a megalomaniac could have imagined the extraordinary success of Coca-Cola throughout the world." Thus, Benjamin Thomas and Joseph Whitehead began the large-scale bottling of Coca-Cola that led to today's massive industry.

For the record, although they became immensely rich, they did not live long enough to enjoy their fortunes. They died rather young, wasted away, it seems, by excessive work. But the pyramid had been formed: behind the Coca-Cola bottlers was The Coca-Cola Company, which supplied the syrup. The structure has not basically changed since. Today the chain is similar in every country where Coca-Cola is sold. The company produces and supplies a concentrated essence to the local bottling firms, who turn it into syrup and manufacture the drink, taking care of their own markets. This structure is one of the main reasons for Coca-Cola's success.

The Hutchinson stoppered bottle — the first Coca-Cola bottle. Opposite: A 1905 magazine advertisement featuring opera star Lillian Nordica.

DRINK
CARBONATED
Coca-Cola
IN BOTTLES 5¢

Chapter 2

BIG BUSINESS

It is often said that the success of a product or personality can be measured by the amount it is imitated. Well-known examples are Vuitton bags, Lacoste T-shirts, Rolex watches, Levi jeans . . . and, for a hundred years, Coca-Cola.

By the dawn of the twentieth century the drink was already so famous that every day new competitors sprang on to the market. Unfortunately, the very name of the drink was easily plagiarized. Neither "coca" nor "cola" were fanciful names, but referred to two natural products, accessible to all. Consequently, imitations were marketed in almost all states. There were "Cokas" and "Colas," ranging from Pepsi, (still a rival today) to Takola Ring,

Cola Congo, Cola Sola, Cola Kola, Cola Nova, Lime-Cola, Ry Cola, Vera Cola, Celery Cola, Better Cola, . . . and so forth.

Benjamin Thomas racked his brains day after day to find a way of making his own drink immediately recognizable, as Pemberton's unique and original formula. He was not helped by the name or the script, as both were so easy to copy and imitate. But it was now too late to change.

He was not helped by the bottle . . . *the bottle*! This was the thing on which to work!

A UNIQUE BOTTLE

After the Hutchinson bottle, a cylindrical bottle had been chosen for Coca-Cola. On it the vaguely lozenge-shaped label stood out in relief, but nobody could say that it was anything special.

Nowadays, the packaging and labeling of a new product is studied by experts in the advertising industry, who carry out sophisticated and extensive market research. It would be unthinkable for a packaging problem to be solved by the manager of an enterprise.

But a century ago, this was not only possible, it happened frequently. When Benjamin Thomas first became aware of the problem, he put his own mind to solving it. He called his business associates together and gave them a speech that concluded something like this: "We must find a bottle that anyone would recognize even in the dark: a bottle unique in the whole world." Such an exclusive bottle used by all Coca-Cola bottlers would consolidate the image of the drink throughout the world.

In 1913 Thomas contacted various manufacturers of glass containers, starting what amounted to a competition to design the future Coca-Cola bottle. A deadline was fixed — three years ahead in 1916. Many and various glassmakers took up the challenge, which could mean, if they won, business of gigantic proportions.

Among them was the Root Glass Company of Terre Haute, Indiana. With feverish excitement, the staff of Root Glass churned out countless drawings of bottles, many with the most extravagant shapes, but all technically impossible to manufacture. Finally they designed the uniquely contoured bottle which we are still so familiar with today; a bottle that recalls the feminine shape, resulting from the hobble-skirts worn in that

period, wide at the hips and tight at the waist and ankle. It was a shape not likely to be confused with that of any other bottle, easy to handle, memorable. As Thomas had wished, this bottle could even be recognized in the dark. It is even registered as a trademark in the U.S. Patent Office. Few other bottles in the world enjoy such distinction.

Later, some people were to see in the shape the generous form of one of the most admired stars of the thirties, Mae West. But it seems probable that the bottle's inspiration came from the commonplace bean of the coca plant. Only after its first appearance did the feminine connection become a popular and intriguing theory for the origin of the design.

What is certain is that the bottle, which has been exhibited in the Museum of Modern Art in New York, made a significant contribution to the growth in sales of the drink throughout the world and to making the trademark so familiar. Mr. Root, after a few years, became the richest man in Indiana.

A chronology of bottles used between 1900 and 1956. At right is a 1915 prototype bottle, presented by a glass company eager for Coca-Cola's business.

Coupon dating from about 1898, handed out at street corners and entitling the bearer to a free sample.

PROTECTING THE NAME

This is the story of the unique Coca-Cola bottle. Apart from the introduction of an enameled rather than embossed name in 1957, it has remained unchanged. King-size bottles and cans have been introduced, but the original bottle has been successful for more than 70 years.

This is an appropriate place to say a few words about the company's patents and the way it protects its products. It is easy to imagine that the protection of its trademark is of prime importance to a multinational company, which for a century has had to contend with innumerable competitors. So it has spent, and keeps spending, thousands and thousands of dollars to guard itself against imitations.

Coca-Cola's success is based on two elements: Pemberton's secret formula and the trademark. If either of the two became public property, it could spell the end of the company. In 1967 the Coca-Cola trademark was valued by experts at three billion dollars. That's not a printer's error — the figure really is *three billion dollars*. That puts in perspective the need for its protection. The American patents system does not make this easy. A couple of well known examples will suffice. Look at why "aspirin" is not an exclusive name in America. Bayer, the original makers, were obliged to abandon it in the twenties, as it was by then considered a noun in common use. The same thing happened to DuPont with "cellophane" and "nylon;" both names were considered to be in common usage. It is easy to imagine what financial damage that caused.

The Coca-Cola trademark was registered on January 31, 1893, when the drink already had quite a wide market and was already being advertised. But the company wanted to protect itself further, by trying to keep exclusive the name "Coke" (as the drink was familiarly called in the States). The fight was hard and came to a positive end only on August 14, 1945 when "Coke" was registered with the U.S. Patents and Trademarks Office. But nothing was achieved for the word "cola," as the High Court regarded it as a generic noun. The Coca-Cola Company is still today continuing its war against competitors, being extremely careful to prevent its trademark from being copied.

DEFENDING THE PATENT

The "giant of Atlanta" also works hard to ensure that the names of its products are always mentioned in the most correct fashion, and, especially with regard to the shortened version "Coke" for which the initial letter C should always be a capital (or "upper case" in printing terms). In this connection, there was an interesting episode concerning the famous writer John Steinbeck. In 1947, in two passages of *The Wayward Bus* he mentioned the name Pepsi-Cola correctly, but not Coca-Cola, which he called "coke," without its capital letter. This was certainly a sign of the fame and popularity of the drink, but the bosses in Atlanta were not pleased, as they were terrified that "coke" might become a generic noun, a term in common usage and therefore of the public domain, and no longer protected as a trademark.

Steinbeck wrote:

"Got any coke?" he asked.

"No," said Breed. "Few bottles of Pepsi-Cola. Haven't had any coke for a month. It's tha same stuff. You can't tell them apart."

The omission of the capital, plus the context of the last two sentences, made them see red at Coca-Cola. So they decided to publish a set of rules and guidelines for the use of their trademarks. This was distributed to journalists, writers, radio and television announcers, disc jockeys, advertising agents, and so forth, under the title *Conversational Guidelines about "Coca-Cola" & "Coke"*. (See illustration overleaf.)

Advertising & Sales Promotion Department

THE COCA-COLA COMPANY

Coca-Cola

MARCHIO REG.

PROHIBITION

In 1919 sales reached a huge 18.7 million gallons of syrup and the company was poised for another surge forward in the crazy twenties. Confused after the First World War, America experienced a very contradictory epoch, characterized on the one hand by enormous economic development pushed forward by the indiscriminate liberalism of Republican presidents, and on the other by acute social conflicts and unjustified fear of revolution. It was an era when great industrial fortunes were made but, at the same time, organized crime and the Mafia became major social problems.

Through it all the romantic advance of Coca-Cola continued, helped hugely by an event that gave the drink a sovereign place in America — the 18th Amendment to the Constitution, dated January 29, 1919, which forbade the manufacture and sale of alcoholic drinks.

Prohibition was born and America divided into two parties, the "Wet" and the "Dry."

Soon there was a third one — the Coca-Cola drinkers. The drink was there: handy, fizzy, refreshing, invigorating . . . and without any trace of alcohol. What a devil was that Pemberton! Had he let a few drops of alcohol slip into his super-secret formula, we would not be reading about Coca-Cola now. The thirst-quenching drink, already widely accepted by those seeking a non-alcoholic beverage, soon became a favorite with all drinkers. It seemed that everyone tasting it for the first time fell in love with it.

"MR COKE"

Yes, they were lucky years for Coca-Cola, but by then the company was being led by a man able to take full advantage of the situation.

In 1919, the Coca-Cola Company was sold by the Candler family for $25 million to Atlanta banker Ernest Woodruff and an investor group he had organized, The Trust Company of Georgia. Soon the business was reincorporated and stock was sold publicly for $40 a share. (Taking into account stock options, splits and dividends one $40 share bought in 1919 would be worth close to $20,000 today!) Woodruff, a financial wizard, had guessed the great potential of Coca-Cola, but he knew very well that to strengthen and widen the market

R.W. Woodruff — the young and charismatic "Mr. Coke".

he had to place a manager with exceptional qualities at the head of the company. A person able to devote body and soul to the enterprise, who believed in and "felt" the product. According to Woodruff's partners, the only man capable of doing the job was his own son, Robert Winship Woodruff. Dynamic Bob Woodruff, 33, had already risen from truck salesman to vice president and general manager of the White Motor Company.

But his father opposed the idea, perhaps because proper professional conduct made him reluctant to push his own son forward. In the end, the view of the other partners prevailed and Bob Woodruff became director of

Two examples of the irresistible progress of Coca-Cola. A 1929 cold-box and (facing page) the very first model of a distribution truck that delivered Coke to some of the most remote parts of the United States.

The Coca-Cola Company in 1923. Thanks to him, the drink became the world-wide leader it is today. Bob became known as "Mr. Coke."

He liked to simplify his strategies within the firm and reduced them to three short "commandments:"

1. Absolute loyalty to the product and the Company.
2. Simplicity of the product (one drink, one bottle, one price).
3. All partners must earn a good salary.

And so it was. From the moment he took over the reins of the company, profits began to grow beyond the most optimistic forecasts. Woodruff was a dynamic person, full of initiative, ideas and enthusiasm, which he managed to transmit to all his employees, from those closest to the most distant. He took care of everything and everybody, from planning the strategies for assaulting international markets, to advertising, quality control and the driving standards of the drivers ("Coca-Cola men must always set a good example in the way they drive . . . "). In just a few years Woodruff went from success to greater success, offering the drink to an ever-growing number of consumers. From the beginning he understood that the future of the drink lay in the bottle and accelerated in that direction. In 1928, for the first time bottled Coke overtook sales of the drink at fountains.

"Mr. Coke's" ambitious drive to sell his product internationally began in 1926 when he founded the

Foreign Department, which in 1930 became the Export Corporation. With hindsight it is easy to judge his initiative as excellent, but at the time Bob Woodruff was risking his own reputation and credibility. He was very careful about quality control, so that in every country the drink had the same standards of quality, uniformity of flavor and taste. Soon, bottling operations were started in many countries, including Belgium, Italy, Mexico, China, Holland and Spain. It was also sold at soda fountains in England, but not bottled there until 1939.

Other important changes sprang from the indefatigable Woodruff. In 1929 the characteristic (though green) Coca-Cola cooler first appeared, followed not long afterwards by automatic vending machines. Young people were immediately captivated. Earlier, what was probably the first six-pack for any drink was introduced in the form of a simple cardboard carton which made it easier to carry more Coca-Cola home.

COMMANDMENT NO. 2 IS BROKEN

For many, many years, point No. 2 of Woodruff's "commandments" was absolutely and rigorously complied with; Coca-Cola was the only product of the company, sold in one package only — the characteristic bottle — and all at the same price.

After the Second World War, these principles began to

crack. A demand was developing from the man in the street for more sophisticated and varied products to suit an ever-broadening range of activities. A small shock was given to the "Giant of Atlanta" by Pepsi-Cola, the eternal rival, which unexpectedly produced a "maxi" package. "Mr. Coke" had to face up to the fact that times were changing.

In the fifties Coca-Cola was not only sold in different packages, but even the manufacture and launch of new fizzy drinks was studied. Fanta was born in 1955 and Sprite in 1961. Although these did not make instant history they are almost as well-known and widely drunk today.

History was made very quickly with a new packaging, the red can, symbol of a new era for Coca-Cola. Metal cans were first developed for the Armed Forces and tested at military installations. They were available to the public by 1960. Their diamond design featuring the hobble-skirt bottle became a familiar sight on market shelves until it was replaced in the seventies with the rip-top can we know so well today.

This was followed not long after by yet another innovation: after years of research into plastic soft drink bottles, The Coca-Cola Company led the industry with the introduction of P.E.T. (polyethylene terephthalate) bottles.

Evolution of the can: From left, 1942, 1960, 1966, and two sizes dating from 1970. Through all the changes, two points remain unaltered: the logo and the colors: Coke's unmistakable red and white.

The Coca-Cola stand at the 1928 Olympics in Amsterdam, first example of sponsorship under Woodruff's leadership.

THE AMERICAN DREAM

Possibly the most credit should go to Bob Woodruff for making Coca-Cola more than just a simple drink. He was a pioneer of, among other things, radio and television advertising, as well as sponsorships. In 1928 Coca-Cola began its association with the Olympics at the Amsterdam Olympiad, where vendors wearing Coca-Cola caps and coats sold the drink to thirsty teams. A thousand cases had been shipped out with the American team.

The dynamic "Mr. Coke" imposed Coca-Cola on the whole of the United States and, little by little, in dozens of other countries. He made the drink his "religion," even preaching that "all the thirsty have a right to a Coca-Cola." And, under his clever leadership, Coca-Cola became a symbol of the American Dream.

The popularity of the drink was scientifically measured in Chicago during the fifties, through an opinion poll.

More than 400 interviewees were shown images — without names — of advertisements of four of the most common products in America at the time:

- a Coca-Cola bottle
- a Ford car
- a Ronson lighter
- a Parker pen

The following are the percentages of people who accurately identified each product by trademark:

64% — pen
75% — car
81% — lighter
99.75% — Coca-Cola

Coca-Cola therefore turned out to be the best known product in the United States.

The triumphant advance continued.

Top: Two 1955 calendar illustrations. Bottom: A 1944 poster.

COCA-COLA GOES TO BRITAIN AND AUSTRALIA

In 1900 Howard Candler, eldest son of the company founder, took a jug of syrup with him on a vacation trip to London. It was served at a soda fountain and an order for five gallons of the syrup was mailed back to the States. But Coca-Cola was not regularly available in Britain until the early twenties when it went on sale through soda fountain outlets that included Selfridges in London and the London Coliseum.

The Coca-Cola trademark was registered in the U.K. in 1922 and The Coca-Cola Company Ltd in 1929, but there was no bottling until 1934 when plants were installed in Chiswick, Southampton, Manchester, Birmingham and Acton.

But then, in 1939, came the war and the company had to withdraw from the civilian market to concentrate its efforts on providing Coke for the North American troops.

With sugar rationing in force until 1953, the return of the British civilian market was slow, but in the early fifties the company's assets were sold to British companies, following its general practice of having local people operate the business.

From being a one-product company until 1955, The Coca-Cola Company now sells more than 250 products and packages, and not only has Coca-Cola become a part of the local way of life but it also contributes to the local economy. In the British Isles today there are 27 Coca-Cola bottling plants, all of them locally owned and operated; and nine Coca-Cola canning plants, of which the Coca-Cola Export Corporation owns only one, which was built to help support the bottlers with their canning needs.

In 1917, a Perth, Australia public accountant, Mr. M F Pye, sought rights to produce Coca-Cola in Western Australia. But the company had no plans for the rest of Australia at that time, and it was not until 21 years later, in 1938, that the first 6½-oz. fluted bottle rolled from the bottling machinery in a small building in Waterloo, Sydney. The first plant had a staff of just 10 and boasted four delivery trucks.

In 1987, Coca-Cola in Australia was 40 years old and bottled in 27 locations throughout the continent. Twenty-six of the plants are now owned by franchised bottlers and the Sydney operation by the company. There is not a city or town where Coca-Cola is not available.

Chapter 3

IS IT JUST A DRINK?

Every night ex-King Farouk of Egypt always expected to find an iced Coca-Cola on the table reserved for him at the best nightclub in Rome.

Emperor Haile Selassie of Ethiopia once sent his royal plane to Cairo, from Addis Ababa, for a few bottles of

The Beatles, ***c.*****1963**

Coca-Cola. And there is a whisper that even in Buckingham Palace there are those who give up the traditional cup of tea in favor of a refreshing Coca-Cola. What is wrong with that?

Coca-Cola has often been available at official ceremonies. For example, President Eisenhower provided it at all the White House banquets. John

Kennedy, the "young" president, drank it; so did Jimmy Carter, who was born in Atlanta and is therefore Coke's fellow countryman.

There have been many heads of state who did not disdain to drink Coca-Cola; the revolutionary Fidel Castro, was once photographed gulping down the drink he had banned a few years before.

Gary Cooper and Marilyn Monroe, Sir Edmund Hillary on his way to conquer Everest, and Chancellor Schmidt of West Germany were all photographed drinking Coca-Cola. For a hundred years millions and millions of people have drunk it — famous and unknown, young and old — people of all races, religions and political beliefs.

300 MILLION IN THE WHOLE WORLD

It can be found in the Marrakesh suk or at Chez Maxim; it can be sipped in the shade of the Pyramids or in a mountain refuge at 10,000 feet. The sun never sets on its kingdom. "Coca-Cola is available all over the world faster than any other natural product, including water" has always been the company's claim. In the United States, Coca-Cola is so in demand that it has more "service stations" than gasoline. Every year in New York alone 14 million crates are consumed. Manufactured in 155 countries, it is drunk every day by more than 350 million people.

It is the most copied drink in the world and the most sold. From the most ferocious attacks and attempted boycotting, it has always come out the winner —"Coca-Cola is indestructible," said Peter Sidlow prophetically. He spent his life collecting advertising signs and objects with the Coca-Cola label. Can one attribute the great success of this drink to its exceptional ingredients? Myth, fad, habit, symbol, monument to consumerism — is it just the world's number one consumer product. Or is it just lucky?

AN IDEOLOGY

Coca-Cola has been used as a symbol of ideologies. Demonstration placards read, "Every bottle is a bullet given as a gift to the U.S. troops in Vietnam!" Accused of promoting American imperialism, Coca-Cola was ferociously attacked and boycotted by the left in 1968. Not only in America, but in other countries too. And yet

Everybody drinks it — Everybody wants it! From President Kennedy to thirsty Arabs in distant deserts.

Coca-Cola, only a few years before, had been ferociously fought against by the extreme right. For example, in Italy Mussolini demanded that people drink Italian soft drinks even though there were already seven local firms bottling Coca-Cola before the war. But by the late 1940s the drink symbolized a new way of life for many people all over the world, becoming a type of status symbol, standing for new attitudes and freedom of thought and debate. The American way of life was filtering through the bubbles.

PATRIOTIC COCA-COLA

One of the reasons why world-wide public opinion came to identify Coca-Cola with the United States government was the close connection between the drink and the Army. And the advance of Coca-Cola in the world was undoubtedly connected with the advance of American troops in the Second World War.

The probably unwitting architects of this advance were Bob Woodruff and General Dwight Eisenhower. The future president, then Supreme Commander of the Allies in North Africa, said, "Without Coca-Cola, soldiers don't shoot!" — and the company's president agreed. After the Allies' landing in Tunisia, Eisenhower hurried to send an historic telegram to Washington in June, 1943: "Send immediately ten bottling-plants." He also instructed that shipments were not to replace military cargo, but at the same time asked for shipment of three million bottles of Coca-Cola!

At once it became a patriotic symbol, helping to sustain morale among the troops. Coca-Cola was available throughout the war on all fronts, even in the front-line. It was a formidable operation, which turned

"The pause that refreshes" brings comfort to the boys in Europe during World War II.

out coincidentally to be an extraordinarily successful advertising campaign.

The success originated from a marketing idea put in practice by the boss, Bob Woodruff. When he was informed that the United States was at the point of intervening in the war, he immediately issued an order, "see that every man in uniform gets a bottle of Coca-Cola for five cents wherever he is and whatever it costs the company." He told his Board of Directors, "Our place is at the front!" And he kept his word.

He took care to justify the need for his drink to be in the daily ration of the troops, through a written document to the government with the meaningful title *The importance of relaxation in the supreme fatigue of war*. Obviously, in the foreground was Coca-Cola, the "pause that refreshes;" symbol of civilian life, of home.

Once he got the go-ahead, Woodruff assembled a team of technicians, "Coca-Cola Colonels", whose duties were to make sure that no soldier went without his Coca-Cola; not even in the most inaccessible place or where the battle was fiercest. Overcoming the most incredible difficulties of transport and supply, the men managed to meet their target. By the end of the war, five billion bottles had been consumed.

But Coca-Cola did more than help troop morale — in many places it gave the local people their first taste of Coca-Cola, and it was a taste that most liked. It put the company in position to take a giant leap forward. In 1940 Coca-Cola was bottled in 44 countries; by 1960 that figure had more than doubled and Coca-Cola had become a symbol of peace the world over.

WAR AND PEACE

Politics have often affected Coca-Cola's life, for good and for bad. In 1968, for example, the drink was one of the victims of the Arab-Israeli war. Coca-Cola was boycotted by the Arab countries (even though it was extremely popular in Lebanon), and had to give up its place to its arch-rival, Pepsi.

A few years later the men from Coca-Cola contributed to the success of the Camp David negotiations, for peace needed trade and earnings.

In 1977 Coke had another bad moment, in India. Faced with the prospect of the bottling plants being nationalized, the company gave up the market rather than risk revealing its secret formula.

But its longest, most complex and exhausting battle was waged to penetrate communist countries. After thirty years of unsuccessful attempts, finally the longed for day seemed to have arrived — the landing on Red Square. Coca-Cola was about to cross the Iron Curtain to the Moscow Olympics of 1980.

Was the epoch of Soviet fizzy drinks, Fruktovava, Gasirovka, Kokta, coming to an end?

Would young Soviets too enjoy the "pause that refreshes?" Would they learn that "it's always Coke time?"

Would a big American star, represented by the capitalist bottle, light up next to the Red Star?

All these questions remained unanswered, for American President Jimmy Carter called for a boycott of the games and The Coca-Cola Company obeyed. This sad episode in the cold war, brought about as a result of the Soviet invasion of Afghanistan, affected not only the athletes, but also that famous American ambassador, Coca-Cola.

No Coca-Cola then for athletes or journalists, who had to make do with orangeade — Fanta; less symbolic but nevertheless owned by The Coca-Cola Company. This compromise saved honor and, in part, business. For Coke, however, the invasion of the Soviet Union was only postponed. Since 1985 a few bottling plants have been producing Coke and Fanta for millions of Tatianas and Ivans.

Coca-Cola cans with labels in Cyrillic (Soviet) script, coming off a canning plant.

Chapter 4

STAR WARS

Other new frontiers were open to conquest by Coca-Cola. Even space itself. In 1985 NASA decided to include a fizzy drink in the astronauts' menu. Displaying the wisdom of King Solomon, they decided the space shuttle Challenger should carry both Coke and Pepsi. This choice displeased the Coca-Cola people in Atlanta, who were irritated at having to deal with competition not only on earth, but also in space.

Earlier, the absence of gravity had seemed an insurmountable obstacle to this type of drink. But Coca-Cola, undaunted, spent $250,000 to design a special container that would allow it to be first into space. The space-can may not externally appear all that different from the one used on earth, but it is in fact a masterpiece of engineering. The liquid is contained in a plastic bag inside a tin can; between the two is a space filled with carbon dioxide. On top there is a totally new kind of lid consisting of a dispensing button, safety valve, flow regulator, nozzle to drink from, and a cap.

It's more difficult to explain than to make.

They thought of every detail, even an adhesive strip, to stick it to the interior of the shuttle, or to the astronaut's overalls, because without gravity the can would float.

It should have been a triumph. But Pepsi intervened to spoil the party. Eternal rivals, Coke and Pepsi have for years been fighting an all-out war for the international market on Earth. They now became arch-rivals in space; however, Coca-Cola *was* the first to be drunk by the astronauts, NASA announced, well aware of the situation.

Opposite: Special cans developed for NASA, for use in a weightless environment.

NEW!
Coke

THE UNMENTIONABLE PEPSI

A climate of intense rivalry has always existed between the two multinationals, though the rumor is not true that the strictest internal rule forbids employees of The Coca-Cola Company from mentioning the name Pepsi in the presence of strangers.

In fact, until very recently, at Coca-Cola they refused to recognize that rivals posed any threat. And yet the war had been going on for almost a hundred years. Pepsi too boasts an ancient beginning, since it came into the world in 1898 in North Carolina. Of its father we know little. It seems he was another pharmacist, Caleb Bradham, who had a drugstore in New Bern. In the first years of this century, seeing the success of Coca-Cola, Bradham decided to devote himself to his own drink, left his shop and founded the Pepsi-Cola Company.

Only recently, after a century, has Pepsi, at least in the USA, worried the management in Atlanta because of the increase in its sales and its young and aggressive image.

"Mr. Coke," in the golden years, liked to say publicly that the presence of a rival served the function of giving "more value" to his drink. And this is true. In the openness of a free market, the presence of rivals certainly can be stimulating. Until the moment it becomes worrying.

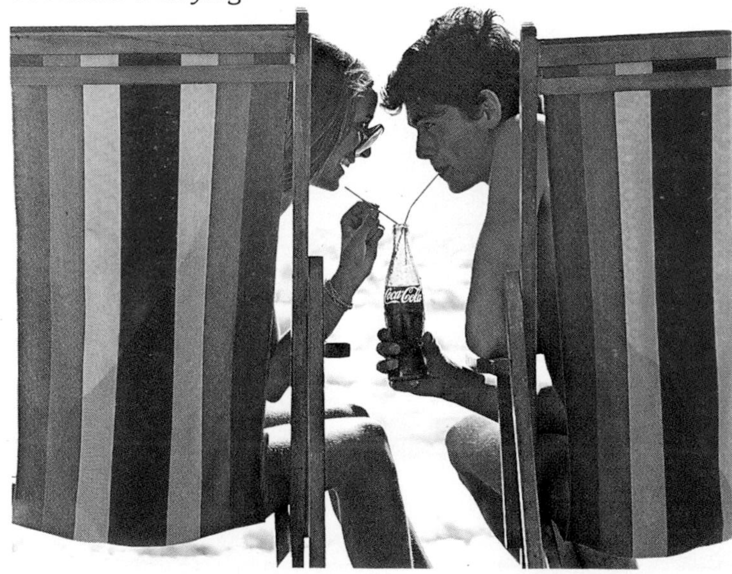

1970s advertisement from a German magazine.

A rose by any other name . . . ! Left to right, top to bottom: English (UK), Thai, Arabic, Russian (Cyrillic style), Amheric, Japanese, Chinese, Hebrew, Korean . . . and English (US).

Next page: Coke at the Great Wall of China.

THE DIVISION OF THE WORLD

Coca-Cola keeps a firm hold on foreign markets and boasts connections with a higher number of countries than the United States government has — today these number 155.

Its strongholds? The Federal Republic of Germany, Japan, Canada, Italy, Brazil, Australia, Latin America. Pepsi found room in the African market, the Middle East and Central Europe. Richard Nixon helped it break into the very difficult Communist market. Before the Moscow Olympics Pepsi had already penetrated the USSR.

Coca-Cola then looked for expansion in China, encouraged by President Carter, who was also from Georgia. Production from the first Chinese plant was to be consumed by an élite of foreign residents and tourists.

The reality turned out to be very different.

The image of the Chinese boy on the Great Wall with the red can in his hand was not a publicity photo, but a snapshot that gives evidence on one hand of the significant changes in Chinese customs all over China, and on the other hand, the bursting force of Coca-Cola.

There is only a limited amount of space in the world, and between themselves, the two multinationals have shared every piece of it. So now, the war between the two companies has moved on to other fronts.

Coca-Cola

HAMBURGER OR HOLLYWOOD

At the end of the seventies, Pepsi decided to enter the fray of a particularly lucrative area, aimed mostly at the young, fast-food market. Frito Lay, Pizza Hut, Taco Bell are some of the fast-food chains bought by Pepsi, with sure instinct. For example, Pizza Hut, bought in 1977 for $300 million dollars, has more than 4000 selling locations in all the United States.

Coca-Cola marked time while its rival devoted itself to commonplace hamburgers and pizza. The "Giant of Atlanta" preferred to invest in researching some rather unusual areas such as prawn and lobster breeding, ocean farming and protein drinks for undernourished populations.

None of these were developed, but Coca-Cola did acquire companies producing wine, coffee and orange juice. The result? In 1980 the soft drink sector represented 76.5% of Coca-Cola's global business. The corresponding figure for Pepsi was less than 40%.

"The future is Pepsi's," boasted the chairman of the company, Kendall. Many careful American savers and stock market investors, liking the diversity of Pepsi's operations, believed the statement and in that year Pepsi's shares reached their all-time high.

The company became galvanised into action in 1981 by a new chief executive, Roberto Goizueta, who had been associated with the Coca-Cola business since 1954, after completing a degree in chemical engineering at Yale.

He worked first for a Coca-Cola subsidiary in Havana, then later in Nassau before transferring to the Coca-Cola Company headquarters in Atlanta in 1964. Elected vice-chairman of the company in 1979, he then became chief executive at only 48.

His first surprise move was the acquisition in 1982 of Columbia Pictures, one of the world's most prestigious film studios.

Pizza for Pepsi, canned dreams for Coca-Cola. Those "dreams" cost $750 million. But notwithstanding some dissenting murmurs ("the film industry is like Russian Roulette; why take the risk?"), Chairman Goizueta was satisfied with, and sure of, his decision. After all, the world of show business and leisure had always been akin to the world of Pepsi. It seems that the company's chairman went for advice to Bob Woodruff, now over 90, who observed, "Let's make sure that people hold a bottle of Coke while watching our films." *Gandhi, Ghostbusters, A Passage to India, A Soldier's Story* — the public had enough good films from Columbia on which to raise a thirst.

Columbia became the cornerstone of the company's entertainment business sector, which quickly developed into new markets like cable television and home videos.

But this high class exploit aside, the chairman of Coca-Cola wanted to launch a stylish attack against his rivals in the main sector, soft drinks. He took his time. After Fanta and Sprite came decaffeinated Coca-Cola, Cherry-Coke and Diet Coke (known as Coca-Cola Light in some parts of the world).

The foods business sector was developed. In 1960 the company had purchased the Minute Maid Corporation, a major marketer of citrus fruit. Coca-Cola Foods was centered in Houston, Texas, and the Minute Maid trademark became its principal brand. Minute Maid had pioneered the production and marketing of the first successful frozen orange juice and under Coca-Cola ownership developed a wide range of frozen concentrated fruit juices and other allied products. Several other brands were also developed including Five Alive, Hi C, Bright and Early; and two coffees, Maryland Club and Butter-Nut.

Then with the impact of a revelation from outer space came the announcement in January 1985 of the NEW COKE.

Opposite: Andy Warhol: Green Coca-Cola bottles (part.), 1962. New York, Harry N. Abrams Family Collection.

Coca-Cola

Chapter 5

100 AND ANOTHER 100

January 3, 1985: the secret

When Barry Day, vice-chairman of McCann-Erickson (the advertising agency that takes care of Coca-Cola's image) entered the underground office jokingly called "the bunker" on Thursday, January 3, 1985, he did not realize that the meeting would mark a historic date. Once the doors were closed, Ike Herbert, executive vice-president of The Coca-Cola Company, and Sergio Zyman, vice-president marketing USA, began by appealing to the sense of honor of those present in order that not one word should leak out about the meeting. Then it took them less than a minute to give the fateful news: the old Coca-Cola would cease to exist and in its place the "New Coke" would be born.

Barry Day remembers the scene: "Everyone suddenly became quiet. For several moments the loudest sound in the room was the noise of the bubbles in our Cokes."

The extraordinary news was totally unexpected by the advertisers, just as it would be to the public at large. The secret had been very well kept in the company, more successfully than many secrets of state. Nobody until that moment had even remotely suspected Coca-Cola, having reached the exceptional goal of a century of manufacture, was to have its historic formula changed, the formula that had led to its extraordinary fortune.

April 18, 1985: the scoop

More than three months went by before the secret plans were exposed. The story was unraveled by an obscure journalist, Jesse Meyers, proprietor of a specialist journal, *Beverage Digest*.

In the issue dated April 19, Meyers announced the change in the Coca-Cola formula. Incredulity and scepticism were the reactions of the attentive and interested readers of *Beverage Digest*. In the United States alone there are about 150 manufacturers of soft drinks behind Coca-Cola and Pepsi. Among these trade readers, the news created an enormous sensation, although it seemed at first to be without foundation.

Enjoy
Coca-Cola
Trade mark ®
Coca-Cola

On Wall street, too, the disclosure was received coldly. "Never change the Coca-Cola formula" had become a Stock Exchange proverb. The Coca-Cola Company protected itself behind a wall of total silence. And many remembered that the old owner, Robert Woodruff, used to say, "They'll only change the formula over my dead body."

But Woodruff had died just a month before.

The rumor continued to circulate with increasing persistence — yet it did not seem to be taken seriously. For Americans the drink familiarly known as Coke is eternal, immutable and unassailable like its contemporary the Statue of Liberty.

What surprises history holds in store!

April 23: big news

However, after a few days an official announcement was made. After 99 years of honorable service, Coca-Cola was to be retired.

The announcement was formally made in the typical American way, with a press conference in Manhattan linked via satellite with the main cities of the United States. The top men in the company introduced the new Coca-Cola, "the Coca-Cola of the twenty-first century." "The king is dead. Long live the king!"

So, were the days numbered for the old, unique formula born of the genial and almost casual ability of the Atlanta pharmacist, John S. Pemberton? It was planned that by the end of summer 1985 it would not be possible to find even one can of the old Coca-Cola in the whole of the United States. And it would disappear without revealing to the world the secret of its formula, so jealously kept for a century.

In fact, the formula is kept in the unassailable vaults of the Trust Company Bank of Atlanta. In one hundred years only about ten people have been near it. It has been said that the only two directors acquainted with the formula always travelled in separate cars or airplanes, in order that the secret would not be lost in the event of an accident.

Is Superman here protecting the precious formula? Certainly Coke's formula is one of the world's most closely guarded secrets. In fact, however, this is a 1971 advertisement promoting Coca-Cola cooler units.

Everybody knows that Coca-Cola is made from a mixture of purified water, first quality sugar, phosphoric acid, natural aromas, caramel, and caffeine. But only three people in the world today know the exact formulation of the super-essence called Seven X, the unique and real base of the drink. And it is the Seven X which is sent from America to all the foreign partners, enabling them to prepare the concentrate on the spot.

A formula that survived a century of history and success was swept away in minutes at the press conference in Manhattan, all its popular and glorious past seemingly finished in a brief moment.

NEW COKE; HOW, WHEN, WHY

At Pepsi-Cola, the news that the old Coke was finished was received with understandable joy. It seemed that at last The Coca-Cola Company had admitted it had difficulties. Advertisements in daily papers throughout America reproduced a statement by the president of Pepsi-Cola which concluded by saying how sweet the victory was and announcing a day off for all Pepsi workers the following Friday. And on the day of the Manhattan press conference, Pepsi really had a ball — they organized a noisy, cheerful street party in the same neighborhood, offering free Pepsi to everyone, even those arriving for the Coca-Cola press conference!

Why ever did Coca-Cola, with sales worth $7.1 billion and a net profit of $629 million in 1984, decide to change its winning horse? It is true that lately in the United States demand had been slackening a little. It is also true that its old rival Pepsi had nibbled away a very small slice of the market. But it was a matter of trifling figures: the global soft drink market amounts to the huge annual figure of $25 billion. Coca-Cola and Pepsi dominate it and Coca-Cola has always been number one. Nonetheless in 1984 the company saw its sales percentage fall from 22.5 to 21.8 despite the introduction of new drinks, while Pepsi gained 0.1%, which corresponds to the not insignificant figure of $250 million, or 77 million crates, each containing 24 bottles.

But can 0.1% justify such a change of course? Was it not rather the growing trend for the youngest American consumers to favor the competition, that alarmed the Coca-Cola managers?

"We were like a great basketball champion playing on his knees. We had the talent, but did not use it. Now we are prepared to take the risk," stated Roberto Goizueta, Chairman of the Board of Directors, 53, with a Yale degree in chemical engineering and an exile from Cuba since 1959. A man described as "a genius of marketing", with an annual cash compensation of more than $1.8 million, a passion for *coups de théâtre* and catch phrases.

What happened was that in the Atlanta skyscraper a decision was made to study a drink with a new flavor to satisfy what appeared to be new trends in the public taste. After being concocted, the new drink was submitted for consumer testing. The tastings took place in great secrecy in both Canada and the United States; 190,000 people aged 13 to 59 were interviewed, without disclosing the source of the drink. Who could have imagined the drink they were tasting could be a new Coca-Cola? The findings seemed to be for the supporters of the new drink: the New-Coke in fact beat the old Coca-Cola 61 to 39. Nothing was left but to prepare the advertising campaign that would announce it to the world.

Happy Birthday, Coca-Cola! And here's to your large "slice" of the mouthwatering soft-drinks market.

diet
Sprite

TAB

diet
Coca-Cola

diet
Coca-Cola

Coke

diet
Coke
100%

diet
Coke
100%
SACCHARIN FREE

Coca-Cola
CLASSIC

cherry
Coke

TaB

Coca-Cola
CLASSIC

cherry
Coke

Caffeine Free
Coke

MARKETING OPERATION

The whole event was conducted in such secrecy (the new red and silver cans had been photographed outside the United States) that not even the independent American bottlers knew anything, nor did those responsible for the foreign branches. Only 24 hours before the great announcement, cryptic telexes were sent from the head office to all the branches world-wide. — "Attention, tomorrow will be a historic day for Coca-Cola!" That was all.

In America the bottlers were summoned to Atlanta the day before and told the news. They had no time to recover from their astonishment, when they found themselves kindly "detained" in their hotel, so that nothing could leak out until the official announcement the following day. Nobody appeared to have the slightest doubt that it could be the most colossal, fantastic, astute marketing operation of the century. Nobody debated the will of the company to make the old Coca-Cola vanish, substituting New-Coke for it.

And this was the reason the operation succeeded. Goizueta had two targets, one with a short-term, the other with a long-term objective. Foreseeing the response of the American consumers to the impact of the news release, he was given an exceptional advertising campaign by the mass media of the Western world, for free. In addition, he livened up sales, close to summer, providing the foundation for further market expansion.

And the facts bore him out: in the warm month of May, in the United States, Coca-Cola recorded an increase of eight points in sales. By the end of 1985, it had gained a total of four extra points in the market, at the expense of the competition.

ALMOST A REVOLUTION

But let us go back. Within 24 hours of the official announcement, more than 80% of Americans knew about the birth of New-Coke. As one journalist pointed out, this was many more than those who knew of Neil Armstrong's lunar walk in July 1969. Consumers rushed to buy the new Coca-Cola, to try the new taste and compare it to the old drink. And controversy started immediately. The new Coke turned out to be sweeter, flatter, and very close to the taste of Pepsi.

A 1942 advertisement in an American magazine.

Its most devoted consumers were disappointed, indignant, even frightened. Thousands of letters of complaint arrived at the Atlanta office. And this was only the beginning. The dailies and the weeklies, as well as television, grabbed the news and expanded the controversy. After only a few days *USA Today* published an opinion poll that showed 59% of consumers preferred the old Coca-Cola, 25% Pepsi, and only 13% the new Coke.

At an interview, the chairman of the company exclaimed, "How come? The new Coke is softer, rounder, more . . . "

"It's not true," retorted the devoted consumers. "This new Coca-Cola has less personality, it's less fizzy; it's like a Pepsi left open!"

"It's a sacrilege!" thundered a lady from Atlanta (who called herself an "alcocacolic"). She rushed to buy as many crates of the old drink as she could find, before it was withdrawn from the market.

In Italy, the wine expert Antonio Piccinardi was given a can of the new Coke to taste. His expert judgment: "Of an amber color, less bright and more intense than the previous one, with a fresher and more penetrating perfume, softer in taste, less sour and slightly sweeter . . ."

Well might those responsible try to calm the consumers. To the Americans Coca-Cola was not the same any more! It was certainly not the same drink with which John Wayne had toasted the landing on Iwo Jima. So said thousands of consumers, by telephone, by letter, on the television, in the bars, in the streets.

"What will happen to my old Cuba libre?" wondered Lewis Grizzard, an Atlanta writer and therefore a compatriot of Coca-Cola. With the new formula being so sweet, the very famous cocktail (three parts of Coca-Cola, one of rum, plus ice) turned out to be totally different, practically undrinkable. The hunt for cans of the old, dear Coca-Cola became frenetic, involving professionals like John Hayden, an attorney from Washington, singers like Al Stewart, caught by the news in London, unknown housewifes from South Dakota, unsuspecting retailers from Texas, students from Yale and Puerto Rican dockers from Brooklyn.

A 1951 poster.

One cry united America, "Don't change the old Coke!" It was just what Chairman Goizueta wanted to hear!

A 1920 magazine advertisement.

TO THE RESCUE

The loudest voice belonged to Gay Mullins, a stubborn pensioner from Seattle who, with his beard and hair speckled gray, vaguely resembled Hemingway. He became in a short time the charismatic chief of the rebellion.

Possibly Mullins himself was part of the extraordinary strategy undertaken by Goizueta. It was probable, but not certain. That Mullins was throwing oil to the flames was a fact; his war declarations shouted to the four winds were excessively exaggerated by the mass media, to the point that they even crossed the Atlantic.

Even authoritative European periodicals published pictures of his pugnacious image, left hand thumb down, brandishing in his right hand an upturned can of New Coke, his face furious and disgusted, while a clever message stands out on his chest which is puffed up with anger. The classic T-shirt which used to bear the slogan "Coke is it!" now read "Coke was it!"

In interviews, this previously unknown citizen of Seattle played on emotions. "They have withdrawn from the market the real Coke, substituting it with something else. Thus they have denied us one of the fundamental rights guaranteed by the American constitution: freedom of choice. Today I am not free to choose any more. Everyone ought to remember well that to define this right we went to war even with Japan."

The indignant citizen, expostulating perfectly the feelings of millions of his fellow countrymen, said, "The

old Coca-Cola is part of the natural landscape of the nation. Changing it would be like painting the White House green simply because green has become the fashionable color." Or, as someone else pointed out, like substituting Brooke Shields' face for Roosevelt's on Mount Rushmore.

Demonstrations were held and were often patriotic in theme. All were in favor of the old Coke, "The only one, the original, the true, the inimitable; not that rubbish that for a few weeks has been usurping a worshipped brand, the very symbol of America."

WILL OUR HERO SUCCEED . . .

Idea: "You don't want to manufacture Coca-Cola anymore? Well then, we will manufacture it ourselves."

From indignation to business is a small step.

In Seattle, Gay Mullins founded the Old Coke Drinkers of America. In about three weeks he received more than 60,000 members. His aims expanded. He bought a share in The Coca-Cola Company and started to write to all the small shareholders, with the idea of attacking the top of the company. And that wasn't all. He called his lawyer and decided to file two legal actions against The

Coca-Cola Company. One was for fraud, as according to Mullins Coca-Cola violated federal laws by putting a new product inside an old container. The other was to compel the company to make the formula Seven X public as "property of the whole country."

As in any respectable American film, at this point there had to be drama. "I have the formula," declared the enterprizing pensioner at the umpteenth press conference. "I can start manufacturing the old Coke starting tomorrow!" If the news was true, everybody wondered how Mullins had succeeded where nobody had in a hundred years. (For interest, it's worth recording that in the sixties Billy Wilder directed a light comedy titled *One, Two, Three*, in which the characters tried in vain to seize the secret of the formula.)

Illustration chosen by TIME magazine for a cover in 1950.

10 JULY: HAPPY ENDING

The American comedy always has a happy ending. And this one couldn't break the rules. Of course, Mullins did not really possess the secret formula, but he had succeeded in ruffling the waters just as much as was necessary.

On July 10, the company issued a statement announcing that, after at least a three months' break, it would start manufacturing the old Coca-Cola again. From then on, in the United States, the label on cans and bottles would include the world "classic," to distinguish the old from the new. So, after all, the original Coca-Cola was allowed to continue on its way.

"We have decided to put the old Coke back on the market," said the bulletin, "because thousands of faithful consumers have let us know that they prefer the old formula."

Gay Mullins and his friends rejoiced. "Long live the old Coke! We've won!", they declared, drinking happily to Coca-Cola's health.

Someone wittily suggested other popular battles. A Washington Post columnist wrote: "We could have back the Volkswagen beetle and milk in glass bottles. For Coca-Cola the future is safe. The legend is undamaged."

"The return to the market of the old Coke seems like a victory of the best American values — democracy from the bottom; spontaneous organization of disappointed consumers, and at the same time a strong sense of tradition and nostalgia," said an article on the front page of the authoritative Italian daily, *Corriere della Sera.*

But people at last began to suspect the whole thing had been a clever marketing operation, conceived to liven sales on the American market.

"Maybe they put the old Coke back on the market a little earlier than expected," an expert commented with hindsight, "but I am convinced that they had some such initiative in the pipeline for a long time."

Journalist Jess Meyers wrote, "If the invention of a new Coca-Cola and the introduction into the market of the old Coke as a new product with the 'classic' label is really the fruit of a well-studied advertising maneuver, then Machiavelli deserves to lose his place in history in favor of Chairman Goizueta . . . "

The bubbles turned to dollars again.

And so the story goes on.

A symbol of friendship: yesterday, as today, the legendary bottle united consumers across the world. This artwork was used in the late 1940s and 1950s to illustrate the international popularity of Coca-Cola.

Symbol of Friendship

Chapter 6

WHAT IS COCA-COLA?

Millions and millions of consumers describe it as "a fantastic drink." An anonymous second-hand car dealer from Memphis, Tennessee, has been drinking 25 bottles a day for 50 years. "It's nice and it's good for you," he said.

"It's very good for you," confirmed a lively 97-year-old woman, who ascribed her longevity to drinking a Coke every morning, at precisely 10 o'clock.

1951 poster.

"It's good for you," according to the Journal of Pediatrics, saying that Coca-Cola reduces intestinal contractions, settling many children's stomach cramps. Many people say that Coca-Cola aids the digestion, others say it is an analgesic. In Brazil some even claim Coke is an aphrodisiac. But above all it has a good effect from a psychological point of view, because for millions of people in the world it has really become "the pause that refreshes." A famous pharmacologist, Robert Klinger, declared that "there is no possibility of toxic effects from this drink, provided it is consumed in moderation by healthy people." For a hundred years Coca-Cola has been drunk by millions and millions of people and has been approved by health authorities around the globe.

NOT ONLY FOR DRINKING

From such an idolized drink, can one expect even miracles? Many legends have blossomed around the supposed properties of Coca-Cola, apart from its thirst-quenching qualities. In the United States some say Coke is useful as furniture polish, a chrome shiner, even as a solution to develop negatives. Some use it as tanning oil, as skin tonic, and some as a contraceptive! In that connection, a report by the Harvard University Medical School made the news by claiming that the old Coke has spermicidal properties superior to those of Diet Coke or New-Coke. That is one of its uses we are not recommending here, just as we do not recommend the substitution of gasoline in your car with Coca-Cola, although this is said to have been done in Jeeps, in emergencies, during the Second World War.

THE INGREDIENTS

WATER

It seems incredible, but it's true that fizzy drinks produced all over the world have the same ingredients: 90% water and 10% sugar.

Water and sugar are the main ingredients of Coca-Cola as well; to these are added carbon dioxide, caramel as a coloring agent, phosphoric acid, natural flavorings and caffeine, according to a formula that is unknown to the public but (as with any other industrial product) known and approved by the health authorities.

The water must be purified to the same standards throughout the world, and all over the world Coca-Cola must have the same taste. To this end, in all manufacturing plants the utmost care is devoted to the water. It is filtered through a system of flinty sands and activated charcoal, becoming lighter, free of the mineral salts that vary in quantity and type depending on the source.

SUGAR

One liter of Coca-Cola contains 4 ounces of cane sugar. Thanks to the acidity of the drink, experts say that the sugar is converted to glucose and fructose, which are both more digestible than cane sugar. However, for those who care about their figure but do not want to give

Water, sugar, carbon dioxide, etc. Plus, of course, the Seven X.

up their favorite drink, today there is Diet Coke, with a negligible calorific content of less than one calorie per 4 fluid ounces (100 milliliters).

CARBON DIOXIDE

This is the gas that gives Coca-Cola its pleasant fizziness and through its bubbles carries more quickly the characteristic flavor to our taste buds. The other function of the carbon dioxide is to prevent bacteria in the air from living in the drink.

CARAMEL

The color of Coca-Cola comes from caramel, which is used in many beverages as well as vinegars, gravies, soups, ice cream, puddings and bakery goods. Actually, homemakers have been making "caramel" in their own kitchens for centuries by heating sugar in a pan. Today caramel color is produced commercially, providing a range of distinctive hues to many different foods.

Coca-Cola syrup at different times in history. Top: In a barrel, 1930. Above left: In a ceramic container, 1900. Right: The concentrate as used by Italian bottlers, c.1950.

PHOSPHORIC ACID
This is one of the many acids such as citric, acetic, malic and lactic acid, used in preparing food or drinks. It not only plays a part in the characteristic bouquet of Coca-Cola, but also serves as a preservative. Phosphoric acid is a natural substance found, for example, in apples, and it is also used in tonics.

NATURAL FLAVORINGS
These are vegetable extracts and essences that form the heart of the Coca-Cola formula. From these natural flavorings comes its unique and inimitable taste. Flowers, fruits, leaves, roots — from each of these parts of the thousands and thousands of vegetable species present in nature we can derive as many extracts and different essences.

Which are the ones used in Coca-Cola? This is the industrial secret that so far has been safely and loyally kept.

CAFFEINE
A bottle of Coca-Cola contains approximately one-fourth the amount of caffeine as a cup of brewed coffee, and about one-third that of tea.

I FEEL . . . FIZZY!

Most people probably do not know who discovered the indispensible bubbles of carbon dioxide, or where or why for that matter. Natural springs of fizzy water were known and valued by the ancient Greeks and Romans, who thought of it as a supernatural gift, and used it both for bathing and as a drink.

In 1767 a British scientist, Joseph Priestley, esucceeded in experimentally mixing water and carbon dioxide to make club soda artificially. In 1772 Priestly himself put together a practical system to aerate water, but it was not until the beginning of the 19th century that the first real plant was established to manufacture fizzy drinks, in New Haven, Connecticut.

Of course, today the technology for producing these drinks is very advanced. But the basic objective is still the same — to capture the bubbles in order to let them burst into life the moment the container is opened.

Chapter 7

LET'S KEEP ON DRINKING

Try saying "Coca-Cola" with your eyes closed. What do you see? The classic bottle, or the red and white can? If you are terribly thirsty does your vision enlarge to the family-size bottle?

Whatever, Coca-Cola came to be presented in many ways to please all its consumers and never leave them dry. An intrinsic part of its history is the story of its packaging, from the development of the original bottle to the metal cans which were first developed for the armed forces overseas.

THIRST INCREASES, SIZES INCREASE

Until the mid-fifties, Coca-Cola was the only drink produced by the Company. It was sold in the 6½-oz. bottle and in draft barrels. But when consumption increased and Pepsi's rivalry intensified (Pepsi surprised everyone with "family" sizes), The Coca-Cola Company decided to diversify its range of bottle sizes while still keeping the characteristic shape. Four new glass bottles were introduced: 10oz, 12oz, 16oz and 26oz. The American public immediately went for them. In the mid-fifties, too, the drink began to be dispensed through pre-mix machines; that is, refrigerators that provided draft Coca-Cola ready to drink. They gradually disappeared during the sixties, and their place was taken by post-mix dispensers, in which the syrup and the fizzy water were mixed at the moment the drink was served, a true production plant at the counter. And it seems that this way of serving the drink (which is almost a return to origins) is winning great favor among consumers.

By 1960 the public was being given the opportunity to buy 12-oz cans. The first were made from three strips of tin plate, but today two pieces of aluminum are used, with the familiar rip-top opening method.

Coca-Cola
MARCHIO REG
Bevete
Coca-Cola
MARCHIO REG

Some bottles were also produced in non-returnable glass, shaped as a traditional Coca-Cola bottle. At Coca-Cola they kept working on new sizes and packages to improve distribution in all countries and led the soft-drink industry with the introduction of plastic bottles in the 1970s.

GLUG GLUG GLUG . . .

American tourists say that when you find yourself at the ends of the Earth and the local bars don't look promising, rather than remain thirsty you should ask for a Coke and drink it from the can. It may not be elegant, but you will safeguard your personal hygiene and also quench your thirst.

In any case, according to the experts, this is the best way to enjoy a Coca-Cola, as they do in the ads. Few things in the world are more pleasant (and more likely to be forbidden by mothers and manners) than to put the glass bottle to your lips and avidly swallow great gulps of the drink, feeling at the same time the light, sparkling tingling in your nose. It's a very pleasant sensation, leaving you simultaneously thirst-quenched and satisfied and yet unsatisfied, as the pleasure ends too soon and so, hopefully, the thirst will return. A Coca-Cola bottle at such times may be too small — for a large thirst a can is better.

But what a difference there is between putting your lips to a sensuous substance like glass and a cold one like aluminum.

Still, the young prefer the can. It has a charm of its own, it is convenient, stable, light; it can be taken wherever you go; it can be opened without any tools — all it takes is to pull the metal ring and . . . pfffff, the drink "breathes out" with its typical sound, signaling to the ear its promise of refreshment.

This is pleasure itself, an altogether different experience from politely pouring Coca-Cola into a glass to drink from. It is more direct, more primitive, and indeed more satisfying — at least, to those eager for maximum enjoyment from their Coca-Cola.

THE STRAW

The very young, however, prefer and indeed often demand a straw, even if this is not the ideal way to taste fizzy drinks — and without mentioning the awful slurping noise it makes at the end!

It was for very young Coca-Cola fans that the colorful, amusing "walky-cup" was conceived; unspillable and just

right for draft Coke. It was an ingenious idea and immediately gained many fans. It is a waxed-paper cup, with a plastic lid pierced by inserting the specially-made straw, which is wider and firmer than the normal kind. You can carry a "walky-cup" wherever you like, and so it is a favorite among tourists and picnickers.

The worst mistake that can be made with this container is to remove the plastic lid and drink directly from the cup, for the paper seems to melt in the mouth and is disagreeable and uninviting, and the drink itself seems to have a different taste. But sucked through its straw in the lid — great Coke drinking!

Кока-Кола
ЗАПАЗЕНА МАРКА
樂可口可
190 ml
コカ・コーラ
190 ml

كوكا كولا
ماركة مسجلة
코카·콜라
190 ml
可口可乐
192 ml

IN BARS, AT HOME, SERVE IT LIKE THIS

Ever wonder why, apart from the obligatory coldness, Coca-Cola does not have a ritual all of its own like tea, coffee, or wine? For even this drink, fast and easy as it is, can be drunk and served even more appealingly.

In a self-service restaurant, one cannot expect more than an ordinary glass or a papercup, an automatic dispenser and optional straw. Order a Coca-Cola in the right bar or coffee house, however, and it might even be presented to you with the respect due to a glass of champagne. To please the eye, the waiter should choose a shiny glass, with a coaster furnished with a napkin, and should pour the drink slowly, to enhance the bubbles to the utmost. The glass must not be warm, as when just taken from the dishwasher, but be at room temperature so the coldness of the liquid straight out of the refridgerator will produce that wonderful film of moisture on the glass. When you pick it up, you anticipate the refreshing taste and, before putting the glass to your lips, you can see for a few more seconds the extraordinary show of bubbles crackling to the top with their unique sound.

1904 magazine advertisement.

To enjoy Coca-Cola at its best, it should be served at 39°F(4°C). Unfortunately, if it has not been refrigerated long enough, it will definitely be less pleasant. No ice should be required, as it is the drink itself that must be almost ice cold. Ice cubes should only be added as a last resort, when Coca-Cola is not at the right temperature and needs to be cooled quickly. Under such

1947 magazine advertisement.

1957 advertisement.

circumstances it's best drunk in one gulp, before it gets too diluted.

And at home? How often have you found yourself in this sort of situation: you have guests, and although you can provide tea or coffee, cocktails or freshly squeezed orange juice, nothing seems to appeal to them . . . coffee prevents some from sleeping . . . tea "not just now, thanks; I only drink it in the morning;" cocktails are too alcoholic; and as for a freshly squeezed juice, "I don't want to put you to any trouble . . . "

Finally, the offer: "Would you like a Coca-Cola?"

"Well, if you've got some . . . I *do* feel rather thirsty!"

And someone else joins the line: "If you're opening a bottle, half a glass, thanks."

Be prepared! They will drink half a dozen *bottles*, one after another, like eating grapes or nuts . . . But among adults, and especially women, who knows why there is a certain reluctance to ask for an ice cold Coca-Cola straight away, as if it were not very refined to do so . . . ?

You must serve the drink following the usual ritual, as

though it were a fine wine. Open the bottle in front of your guests and pour it into crystal glasses. For guests, avoid using family-size bottles and cans — keep these for children's parties or for daily use. The glass bottle is certainly more pleasant to the eye and has the advantage of being consumed all at one time, thereby allowing you to offer a newly opened bottle every time a glass needs refilling.

IS THERE ANY DIFFERENCE?

Baldovino Ulcigrai, the Italian journalist and wine expert, was asked to answer an interesting question: Is there any taste difference between Coke in a can, and Coke from a plastic family container? Many Coke-lovers claim to be

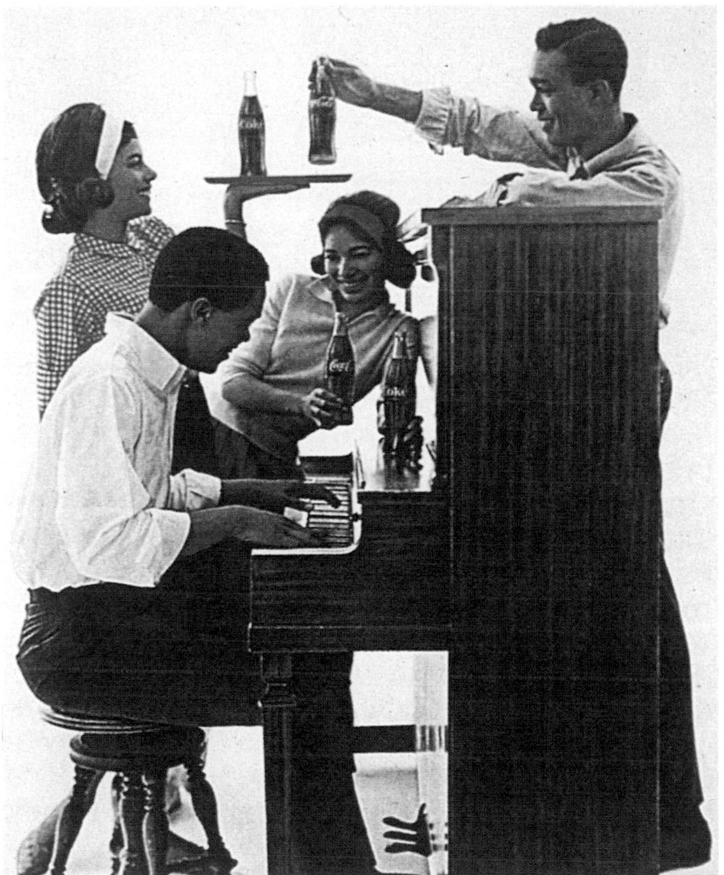

1963 advertisement

able to distinguish simply by taste, with their eyes closed, a Coca-Cola in a can from one in the family bottle. Is this true?

Ulcigrai's test followed the rigorously applied method of wine-tasting even though the expert was unsure that the laws of wine tasting would be effective when sampling a drink so different from wine.

The chosen samples were: — a 1.5-liter (50 fl.oz.) plastic bottle (labeled "A"), and a 330 ml (11 fl.oz.)can (labeled "B").

There was no noticeable difference in appearance, for color and clarity were both the same dark amber color, clear and transparent. The olfactory test showed sample "A" to have the characteristic, expected smell, while sample "B" appeared to have a more delicate bouquet. As for taste, "A" was delicately agreeable, with a dry aftertaste, slightly acid and not full-bodied; "B" was slightly fuller, pointed,and kept its fizziness longer, which is significant, considering the two containers had been opened at the same time.

Are people right who maintain there is a difference between Coca-Cola in plastic bottles and Coca-Cola in a can? Not in theory, as when the drink comes out of the bottling plants, in whatever package, it has absolutely the same taste. What differences are found could be due to the way in which the containers have been kept up to the time of tasting. For example, the plastic container does not protect the drink from light which might have caused the slight difference detected by the expert. But he concludes, "For reasons of tradition and pleasure to the eye, I would choose neither A nor B but Coca-Cola from a glass bottle, which is generally preferred for sentimental reasons."

The tasting took place on November 28, 1985. But note the samples served were at room temperature and you are advised never to do this. As said before, Coca-Cola should be served at 39°F(4°C)!

A SLICE OF LEMON?

What should you say to the offer of a slice of lemon in your Coke at a bar? Does lemon go with Coca-Cola?

Again, Baldovino Ulcigrai was asked. Sample "C" was made by adding a slice of lemon to sample "B". To the eye there was no difference, but to the nose "C" had a definite and agreeable citrus smell.

And the taste? The expert found that the acidity of the lemon did not add briskness to the product, which became altered, especially at the tail end. So the answer? If you prefer the perfume to the taste, go for the slice of lemon; otherwise drink your Coke straight, to ensure its characteristics are unchanged.

1981 advertisement in German.

Chapter 8

THINGS GO BETTER WITH . . .

Coca-Cola, a famous slogan claims, can accompany any dish, sweet or savory, spicy or delicate, of any cuisine. And even if not all gourmets agree with this claim, there are millions of people throughout the world prepared to stand by it. People drink it soon after waking up, with their breakfast, before bed, at restaurants, at parties, during work breaks, in the car, at school, at meetings, always and everywhere.

Things are different in Europe — for example, in Italy, homeland of the meal of many courses, land of fine wines, epicures approve of Coca-Cola only when it accompanies fast foods like sandwiches, hamburgers, pizza.

We cannot expect them to approve if we order a cool Coca-Cola with a *filet maître d'hôtel*, seafood or roast of beef.

Even so, this flirtation with Coca-Cola is on the increase. Market research has shown that the consumption of this drink is higher in workplaces where people work shifts, which forces quick meals and snacks. Young people, born in the Coca-Cola "boom", urban and vital, are used to sipping the drink at any moment of the day, having it always ready in the refrigerator, accompanying with ease a soup, pasta, steak or fish. Some swear that the ideal drink to have with smoked salmon is Coca-Cola, because the smokey flavor perfectly complements the sweet acidity of the beverage. You have to try it to find out!

COCA-COLA IN THE KITCHEN

Few know that Coca-Cola can be used in the kitchen for preparing special dishes. Culinary experimenters have given their opinion after long research and tastings, and this is their judgment: the drink is excellent in introducing a spicy touch, an extra, decisively pleasant note to sweet-and sour recipes. Here is one very well-known recipe for an exquisitely tasty dessert which has a reputation as an aphrodisiac.

EXOTIC PINEAPPLE WITH COCA-COLA

8 slices of pineapple, 35 fl.oz. Coca-Cola, one lemon, a small glass of rum; sugar, whipped cream

Marinate the pineapple in Coca-Cola for a couple of hours, with the sliced lemon. Then add a teaspoon of sugar. Add a little Coke to the rum, pour over the pineapple slices, and serve with whipped cream.

With Coca-Cola new, unusual ice cream recipes can be invented by mixing it with fresh fruit, especially peaches, apples and strawberries.

PEACH GELATO

9oz peaches, 14 fl.oz. Coca-Cola, 4oz sugar, strawberries, gin.

Blend the flesh of the peaches, after taking the stones out and peeling them, adding 7 fl.oz. water and Coca-Cola, in which the sugar has been dissolved. Put in freezer for 20 minutes. Serve decorated with strawberries and with a drop of gin.

COCA-COLA "GRANITA".

12 fl.oz. Coca-Cola, 1½ oz.sugar, lemon juice.

Mix all together and freeze, then liquidize at a low speed. You can substitute the lemon juice with grapefruit juice.

COCKTAILS AND LONG DRINKS

Coca-Cola is king of the long drinks, which is not surprising as these were born in America. Legend says that the term "cock-tail" was originally coined by an American woman, Betsy Floyagan, a canteen-keeper for a cavalry regiment in the early 1800s.

Among the most famous inventors of cocktails, long drinks and aperitifs, we must remember another American, Robert Crosley, "father" of all bartenders, to whom we owe the famous Manhattan, Brazil, Parfait.

We know nothing, though, of the inventor of the most famous long drink based on Coca-Cola, the Cuba Libre, which certainly was already widely made before being recorded for posterity.

Coca-Cola in fact lends itself perfectly as a mixer for rum, whiskey or vodka, with nothing else needed. A well-used trick at parties is to go around with a glass of Coke in your hand. If you want to drink a strong drink without letting on, the glass is filled half with whiskey. If you prefer not to drink, simply fill right up with Coke and pretend to be savoring a Cuba Libre!

It was the Cuba Libre that caught on among teenagers at parties in the sixties. It had the exciting flavor of rebellion!

Here for you is a selection of thirst-quenching and pleasant drinks. All recipes require the ingredients to be poured into a tumbler.

CUBA LIBRE

Half-fill a large shaker with crushed ice and add:

one teaspoonful sugar, juice of half a lemon, one measure of rum, lemon rind

Fill with Coca-Cola, mix and serve.

HULA HOOP

Pour in a large shaker:

1/2 measure lemon juice,one spoonful of sugar, 1/2 measure dry gin, ice

Fill with Coca-Cola, mix and serve with a slice of lemon.

YANKEE

1/4 whiskey, 3/4 Coca-Cola

Serve in a large glass with ice cubes and a slice of lemon.

WESTERN

1/4 gin, 3/4 Coca-Cola

Serve in the glass with ice and a slice of lemon.

Coca-Cola
MARCHIO REGISTRATO
Bibita analcoolica. Ingredienti:
acqua, zucchero, anidride
carbonica, colorante caramello
acidificante acido ortofosforico
aromi naturali, caffeina.
Da consumarsi preferibilmente
entro la data indicata
sul fondo della lattina
Contenuto 50 cl

NEGRITA
1/2 pineapple juice, 1/2 rum, Coca-Cola

Mix in the shaker with ice and finally add Coca-Cola

HEAD
Pour in a large shaker:
50% rum, 20% grapefruit, 30% banana Bols, ice.

Fill with Coke, mix and serve.

TATUILA
Pour in a large shaker:
15% banana Bols, 15% mandarin liqueur, 50% rum, 20 % grapefruit juice, ice.

Fill with Coca-Cola, mix and serve garnished with cucumber balls.

EL SOL
1/2 crushed ice soaked in Fernet or mint Fernet, 1/2 Coca-Cola

Serve in a large glass with lemon peel.

VENETIAN
1/2 red vermouth, 1/2 Coca-Cola

Serve in a large glass with ice and lemon peel.

OPTIMIST
Pour in a large shaker:
1/3 brandy, 1/3 white Curacao, 1/3 Coca-Cola, juice of 1/2 lemon, ice.

Mix and serve.

RUSSIAN
1/4 vodka, 3//4 Coca-Cola, ice.

Serve in a large glass with lemon peel.

WANTED

Pour in a large shaker:

10% lemon juice, 10% orange juice, 10% grapefruit juice, 10% Triple Sec, 60% rum.

Fill with Coca-Cola, mix and serve garnished with a slice of banana.

FRUIT LONG-DRINKS WITH COCA-COLA

ELOISE

1/2 avocado, 2 tablespoons Cointreau, 2 fl.oz. rum, Coca-Cola.

Blend avocado with Cointreau and three ice cubes, pour in a large shaker with the rum and Coca-Cola. Mix and serve, garnished with a slice of kiwi fruit.

GAIA

1 persimmon, 2 teaspoons Grand Marnier, 2 fl.oz. rum, Coca-Cola.

Blend the persimmon with the rest of the ingredients, then pour in a large shaker, add Coca-Cola and serve. Garnish with slices of exotic fruit.

MONICA

1 apple, 2 fl.oz. lemon vodka, 1 strawberry, Coca-Cola, 3 ice cubes

Blend half an apple with vodka and ice; pour in a large shaker and add Coca-Cola. Mix and serve garnished with the strawberry.

MARCO'S

2 slices melon, 2 fl.oz. sherry, Coca-Cola, 3 ice cubes

Blend melon, sherry and ice. Pour in a large shaker and add Coca-Cola. Mix and serve, garnished with a slice of melon.

SONORA

60% peach juice, 40% Grand Marnier, Coca-Cola.

Mix in a shaker with ice, adding Coca-Cola last.

Nowadays, special teas are very fashionable. Thirst-quenching, digestive, curative, they are the ideal drinks for those who cannot stand alcohol. We propose this simple recipe based on Coca-Cola, which will be welcomed by those who want something different, but not too elaborate.

FRESH COCA-COLA

1 bottle Coca-Cola, fresh mint.

Marinate the mint in Coca-Cola, in a jar. Use about ⅓ oz. mint to each liter of Coca-Cola. Leave for one day in the refrigerator. Serve with ice.

To avoid losing the drink's fizziness, insert the mint leaves inside the bottle and cork it immediately.

A successful international advertising campaign revived the yo-yo, which was used as a premium.

Chapter 9

"COCACOLAMANIA"

According to its most ardent fans, Coca-Cola overcomes all fears, even the fear of death. In August, 1976 the *Louisville Times*, announcing the death of J.P. Day, reported his last words as: "I'm dying in peace, because I know in Heaven, too, I'll find Coca-Cola."

Day was not the only one to believe in the immortality of the famous drink. The Californian collector, Sidlow, who once owned the world's best private museum consecrated to Coca-Cola, placed a bottle, with great care, in a fallout shelter.

Will this symbol of our civilization survive a nuclear holocaust? Film director Marco Ferreri thought about that. Toward the end of his film *Il seme dell uomo*, (*The Spirit of Man*) the two survivors of a nuclear holocaust see something appear in the sky, a sort of airship, ill-defined in shape. When they suddenly realize it is an enormous Coca-Cola bottle, one cries out, with a sigh of relief, "In that case, New York must still exist!"

GADGETS' PARADISE

Since the beginning, the advertising of Coca-Cola has been intensive and creative. Dozens and dozens of objects bearing the Coca-Cola name were distributed among traders and consumers. These pieces, some unquestionably beautiful, are much sought after by collectors, who are often prepared to pay high prices for them.

In the beginning, such promotional merchandise was not co-ordinated by the Coca-Cola Company. Each bottler could act freely, according to his needs and taste. Hence, at times, a rather bizarre range of objects have been manufactured, some even questionable; like razor-blades, which hardly projected the desired Coca-Cola image.

Candler was the first to tackle the problem of coordinating this rapidly growing sideline. Records kept since 1913 show that Coca-Cola has distributed millions of advertising objects; for example, 5 million posters, 60,000 ornaments for dispensers, a million calendars, 5000 artistic glass lamps, 10 million matchboxes, 50,000 thermometers, 20 million notepads, 50 million paper napkins, and so forth.

It was Bob Woodruff who, in 1924, finally managed to establish a co-ordinating committee, which aimed to

prevent the bottlers from developing promotional material independently. But it was not until 1982 that a formal merchandise licensing program was established. Its prime objective was to protect the Coca-Cola and Coke trademarks. Today, legal approval must be obtained before the trademarks can be used on any merchandise. There is also a standardization committee, which controls the appearance of goods used by the bottlers in their daily business — the design of uniforms, trucks, cases, letterheads, etc.

There is an official Coca-Cola museum on the ground floor of the company's headquarters in Atlanta, where hundreds of objects are displayed. Of course, they are all original. But, as always happens, innumerable copies and imitations have been made; however, even some of these are of value to the collector.

America's recorded history is certainly shorter than that of Europe, and this may be the reason why a humble 1900 Coca-Cola bottle may be preserved with more care than many great works of art in Europe.

Trays and coasters from the beginning of the century — just three of the many objects sought by Coca-Cola enthusiasts.

Next page: A private collection of Coca-Cola memorabilia.

PROVIDED IT IS SIGNED COCA-COLA

Coca-Cola advertising gimmicks are certainly not "art" in the true sense, nor are they truly representative of our culture, but they are important evidence of twentieth-century human activity, for they are products of applied art and technology, symbols and relics of our time and our civilization.

So, by examining them, one can find even through Coca-Cola gadgets a key to better understanding of the age just gone. In this respect, calendars are possibly the most interesting. They were often illustrated by famous artists like Norman Rockwell, and much can be learned from them about fashion, the treatment of women, and social customs of the times. However, the most fanatical collectors gather with the same passion the most beautiful posters and trays, together with wooden crates, paper cups and bottle caps.

Coca-Cola
TRADE MARK REGD.
Coca-Cola
Coca-Cola
Coke

FERNSEH
Coca-Cola
Grazie!
Coca-Cola
Coca-Cola
TRINK
Coca-Cola
Coca-Cola
REGISTERED TRADE MARK

FROM CIGARS TO TRUCKS

The collectors' bible is *The Illustrated Guide to the Collectibles of Coca-Cola*, by Cecil Munsey. A book of more than 300 pages, it lists the most representative promotional objects, from the oldest to the most recent (usually up to 1970), from the most common to the most extravagant. These are not just limited to traditional bar furnishings; alongside glasses, paper napkins, calendars, trays and ashtrays, we find cigar bands (dating from 1927 to 1944); Gillette razor-blades (dating from 1910; very few of these are still left), and spearmint chewing gum (signed Coca-Cola).

The true collector will diligently search for puzzles, yo-yos, paperweights, coasters, bottle openers, clocks, pencil sharpeners, lighters, radios, key-rings, wallets, toasters, and will stop at nothing just to have a sign, an automatic dispenser, or a two-meter-high maxi-bottle. If he has the money, he could even aspire to an 1898 tray, for which the owner was recently offered about $15,000; or if he has room in his garden, a truck used to transport Coca-Cola in the forties. A refined collector might prefer to devote himself exclusively to the educational material sponsored by Coca-Cola — portraits of presidents and other great men, maps and airplane posters.

True fans are envied, not only for the quality of their collection, but also the quantity.

John Buchholz, of Atlanta, has a room with a Coca-Cola carpet on the floor, Coca-Cola curtains, Coca-Cola bedspread, Coca-Cola drinks trolley, Coca-Cola trays hung on the walls and six shelves filled with Coca-Cola glasses and bottles. Another anonymous collector transformed his attic into a cheerful warehouse of Coca-Cola objects, an explosion of red and white, where the characteristic trademark appears countless times, like a set of mirrors.

Coca-Cola . . . where is the secret of its charm? "It's like with a beautiful woman," sighs a fan. "One falls in love without knowing why."

Chapter 10

THE BUILDING OF THE IMAGE

Any product, object, or person can emerge from obscurity to become a renowned personality or a household word. Some examples come easily to mind: Coca-Cola, Marilyn Monroe, the Beatles and Campbell's soup. What are the reasons for their almost immortal success? How does the obscure girl become the divine Marilyn, leaving behind thousands of aspiring stars, even more beautiful, more highly educated, better trained? And why has Coca-Cola bumped dozens of competitors on its way?

It is not just a matter of the validity of the product, or the marketing strategies, or well-trained management. To be transformed from some obscure object into a legend, a product needs an intelligent publicity campaign, carried out continuously, concentrating on the positive values in order to captivate the consumer. The legend, in fact, says Roland Barthes, is not the message so much as the way it's delivered. Coca-Cola therefore drew attention to itself and its place in the sun through the rituals of modern communication, which it was always able to exploit fully, to its own advantage.

Nonetheless, it is quite clear that not even advertising campaigns which hit the nail right on the head could alone explain the success of Coca-Cola. In all great legends, there is a certain indefinable something that is above all rules and theories. In human beings, it is called charisma.

The personality of a product is formed by a gathering of different elements: name, packaging, price and advertising . . . plus that extra "something."

DRINKING AN IMAGE

Why does somebody drink Coca-Cola rather than just any other drink? Is it perhaps because the rival products have been tried and comparisons made? In 99% of cases the answer, of course, is no. People drink Coca-Cola because they identify perfectly with the image Coca-Cola projects to its consumers. They choose to drink

Coca-Cola not only for the intrinsic quality of the product, but beyond that, for the image the drink creates.

A 1940s-1950s promotional character known as the Sprite Boy.

The famous American advertising agent David Ogilvy said, "Give someone some Old Crow to taste and tell them it is Old Crow; then give them another glass of Old Crow, but tell them it's Jack Daniels. Ask them which they prefer, and they'll tell you the two are very different. In effect they were tasting images. "In building an image," continues Ogilvy, "every statement must carry the same message; the advertising of a product must constantly project the same image, year after year."

Not everybody agrees, especially the clients of advertising agencies, who are frequently eager to change advertising campaigns every season. For Coca-Cola, however, the principle has proved to be valid and successful. The Coca-Cola approach, with the unusual continuity of its message, is quite rare in advertising history. From the day in May, 1886, when Pemberton decided to advertise his new drink in the local newspaper, and described Coke as "delicious" and "refreshing," little has changed. Going through the lucky slogans which have gradually evolved to advertise the drink, it is surprising to find the basic concept is always the same: it is refreshing, one of the things that makes life pleasant; it is a mark of hospitality and friendship. From "Delicious! Refreshing!" in 1886 to "Wherever you go" in 1905, to "The pause that refreshes" in 1929, to ". . . it's the real thing" in 1942, to "Things go better with Coke" in 1963 to "Coke is it" in 1982 — all have the same theme.

Maybe the most significant difference is between the $46 spent in 1889 by the old apothecary and the multi-million-dollar budgets of recent years.

It is not only a matter of money, of course. There have also been some changes in the intervening years, above all to the consumer image. The visual part of Coca-Cola advertising has always been up-to-date and shows the present exactly as it is at that very moment; a very realistic slice of life in which it is possible to identify habits, fashions, social customs. Looking at Coca-Cola advertisements is like reading so many years of American history — although, like Hollywood movies, it is seen through rose-tinted spectacles.

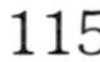

"Delicious and Refreshing." In 1926, six million drinks of Coca-Cola were sold daily. Atlanta well knew the importance of time and of advertising.

IN HOLLYWOOD THEY DRINK COCA-COLA

Since the very beginning Coca-Cola has made use of testimonials from very famous people, from the opera singer Lillian Nordica to the homely Hilda Clark. But the golden era of advertising coincided with Hollywood's golden era. Celebrated stars, idols of the crowds, men and women who peopled the dreams of millions and millions of Americans willingly agreed to lend their smiling faces to the Coca-Cola "pause." At Coca-Cola they realized consumers would identify the success of their favorite idols with the use of the drink, awarding equal success to both company and star. It was a real triumph. From Johnny Weissmuller, the most famous movie Tarzan, posing next to Jane, Maureen O'Sullivan, to the platinum blonde Jean Harlow. Few stars would not pose for the master poster artists like Hamilton King. They appeared on posters, calendars and trays in the thirties and forties, drinking their Coke, delighted.

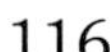

Testimony from the stars on this 1934 tray — Johnny Weissmuller and Greta Garbo. Opposite: Garbo; and Joan Crawford, who later married the President of Pepsi.

Coca-Cola
Greta Garbo

Coca-Cola
Joan Crawford

Joan Crawford did it too — and therin lies an unusual and bizarre story. She married the company's Vice-President, Alfred Steele. Later, after a bitter disagreement he left Coca-Cola and joined Pepsi-Cola, becoming President. When in 1959 he died suddenly, Joan became a director of Pepsico and played a very active part in public relations for Pepsi-Cola. Not many stars had campaigned for both!

Using film stars in advertisements brought great fame to Coke. Let us not forget that those were the golden years of Hollywood, the huge dream factory. Coca-Cola managed to fit perfectly with these dreams — all-American, brimming with good feelings, with success, money, love and heroism. The drink assumed a whole series of values, through a positive identity that never failed. By drinking Coca-Cola, "I can become like . . . "; or "certain things can happen to me while drinking a Coke."

FROM MEDIA TO MASS-MEDIA

What would Piccadilly Circus be without its brightly lit advertising signs, including the one for Coca-Cola? The Coke people in Atlanta were always drawn by novelties and were among the first to use electricity, lighting Times Square in New York with the name Coca-Cola, and gradually many other squares, more or less well-known, all over the world. Today there are more than twenty million billboards, their flashing lights reminding us of the drink from one side of the world to the other.

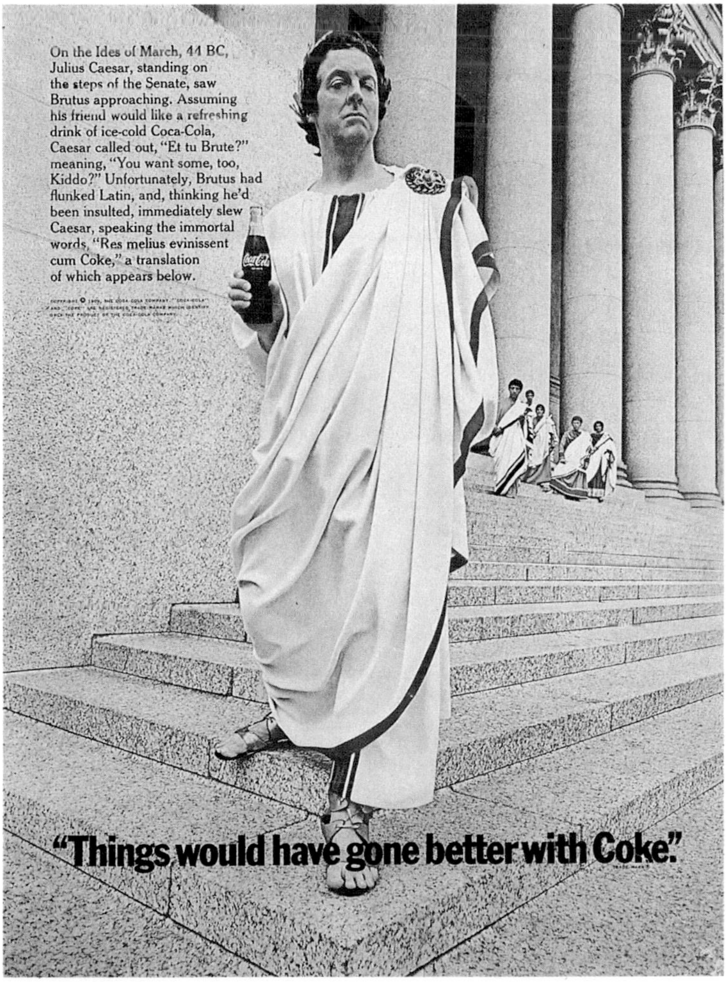
On the Ides of March, 44 BC, Julius Caesar, standing on the steps of the Senate, saw Brutus approaching. Assuming his friend would like a refreshing drink of ice-cold Coca-Cola, Caesar called out, "Et tu Brute?" meaning, "You want some, too, Kiddo?" Unfortunately, Brutus had flunked Latin, and, thinking he'd been insulted, immediately slew Caesar, speaking the immortal words, "Res melius evinissent cum Coke," a translation of which appears below.
"Things would have gone better with Coke."

60 80 100 140
DRINK
Coca-Cola
ICE COLD

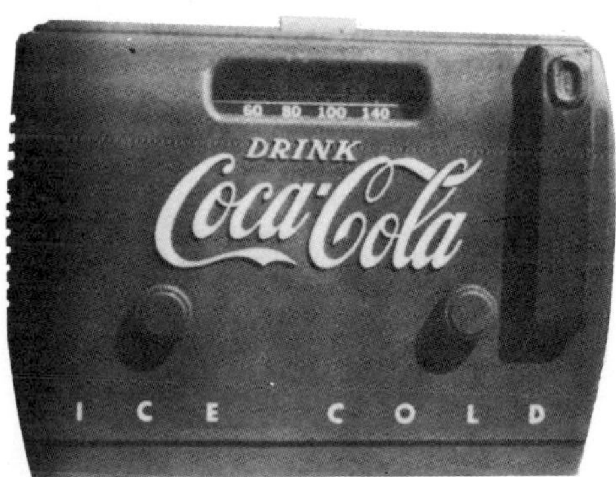

Above: One of a 1969 series of magazine advertisements parodying historic occasions. Left: A dealer-loader premium from the late 1940s.

Credit for the first large Coca-Cola advertising campaign definitely must go to President Woodruff, who was gifted with remarkable perception with the media, and also to the more obscure Archie Lee, a member of staff of the D'Arcy Company, the agency that managed the company's budget from 1906 to 1956. "In every refrigerator a bottle of Coke" was the agency's aim epitomized by their slogan "within an arm's reach of desire." They succeeded. To do so it was necessary to reach an ever-widening class of consumer, with a coordinated campaign through all available media.

Starting in 1904, prestigious advertisements were placed in the main papers that had influenced a restricted group of the population — the educated and rich. And that had a spin-off effect on those who aspired to that lifestyle. The point of sale, still today one of the most important areas of sales promotion, was regarded as especially important. So was a whole series of promotions, including free samples and gadgets such as calendars, posters, pens, postcards and so on, which

became museum pieces and collector's items. But to reach the broadening target, Coca-Cola needed more universal vehicles for promotion. These were found in the radio, the first communications system to reach the real mass market. In a very short time it spread very widely through the population, which could not be reached through the printed word. The first radio program sponsored by Coke was broadcast in 1927. On 14 stations of the National Broadcasting Company the "voice" of the drink was heard over almost the whole United States of America. It was the beginning of a new era.

THE GOOD LIFE

Who can deny that a person is happier if he can drink a Coca-Cola whenever he feels like it? It is a fact that in the twentieth century people have a growing preoccupation with themselves; with the satisfaction of their own material and spiritual wishes and aspirations, with their own needs, whether real or imagined, and towards the pursuit of their own leisure and pleasure.

Beauty, youth, energy — three main themes of the Coca-Cola image.

After the Second World War, this tendency steadily gained strength. Cars became affordable to many more, houses more and more comfortable. Thanks to modern gadgets, life became generally easier, work less heavy. The good life became a reality for millions and millions of families, even for those who, before the war, were far from affluent American society. Coca-Cola needed to adapt to these big changes in the lifestyle of its consumers. A bottle in every refrigerator was not enough — everybody had to *have* a refrigerator!

Just when it became necessary to steer a new course, Archie Lee died and the agency could not find as creative and able a replacement. After half a century of successes, the Coca-Cola Company felt obliged to leave the old D'Arcy agency in 1956 and assigned its budget to the emerging company, McCann-Erickson (now a world giant), which had won distinction through an interesting campaign for Esso.

And McCann (especially the "Four Musketeers" of advertising, Paul Foley, Neal Gilliat, Bill Backer and Stewart Brown) projected Coca-Cola's image in the right direction.

THE WORLD BELONGS TO THE YOUNG

The new epoch meant new consumers, and after a detailed analysis of the market and emerging social phenomena, McCann decided to divide their target markets into segments and to concentrate on teenagers during the sixties.

So the youth phenomenon, which exploded with such impact world-wide in the 1960s, was anticipated by the ad men. Coca-Cola became a symbol of youth.

Still following the overall theme of previous advertising campaigns, the agency made an important change in the direction of images and language by directing the main thrust of its promotion through the new medium of television. Although radio and other media continued to be used strongly, after the fifties Coca-Cola's growing budget was invested predominantly in television commercials. The new mass medium, with its extraordinary influence quickly became the most suitable for the product. Coca-Cola — the "champagne of the young" — became more and more a symbol of their way of life.

Love — Happiness — Holidays; the young and their world, a constant focus for the Coca-Cola message.

Above: A 1986 advertisement in Spanish.

And in this change of language, image and rhythm, music became of prime importance. From the Hollywood stars of the thirties and forties, our drink moved on to the new idols, pop singers. The greatest pop stars of the time were engaged for the jingles; from Ray Charles to Tom Jones, from Nancy Sinatra to Neil Diamond, from Petula Clark to Aretha Franklin.

Right: A poster featuring jazz singer Aretha Franklin, *c.*1970.

RETHA
COMES ON FOR
COCA-COLA
ONLY 50¢ AWAY FROM YOUR WALL
And waiting for a very vertical place of honor. This bedazzling 16" x 27" pop art poster of Aretha Franklin for your collection.
Just send 50¢ to:
POP POSTERS, P.O. BOX 5377, GRAND CENTRAL STATION, NEW YORK, N.Y. 10017
(Make check or money order payable to "Pop Posters.")
NAME
ADDRESS
CITY
STATE
ZIP
Coca-Cola

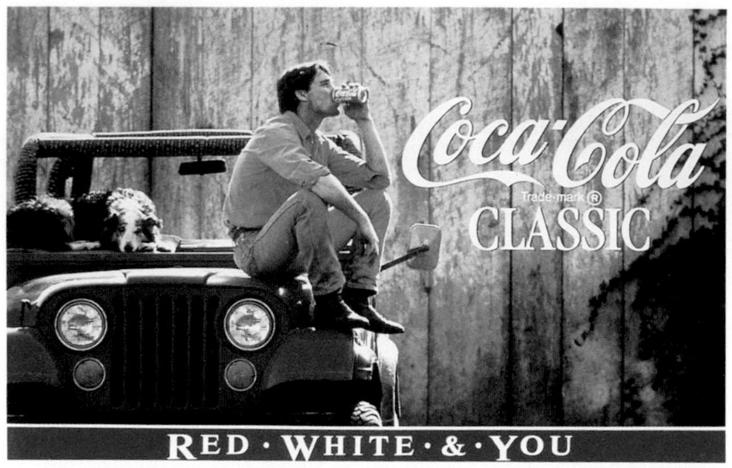

Above and opposite: Three 1986 advertisements.

"It's the real thing." — and just as real and important was the emerging phenomenon of the new generation.

From America to the British Isles, from France to Australia, to all the other countries where Coca-Cola could be bought, teenagers, with their awakening consciousness, spoke a language epitomized by the image of Coca-Cola as now presented by the advertising agents.

WITHOUT FRONTIERS

In the seventies the climate had changed; it had become more thought-provoking and much more difficult. The great enthusiasms were extinguished, having clashed with a reality very different from that promised by a bottle in the sixties. Vietnam, terrorism, economic crisis — these were the realities of the time; a very recent, not-yet-forgotten past.

Those were the years when Coca-Cola was ferociously attacked. Once more the image needed to be adjusted. The wizards at McCann took care of it. Coca-Cola was presented as a universal drink that united the young without distinction by race or creed. Gone was the time when two separate ads were designed which were identical, except for white models in one and black in the other. Black, brown, yellow, white; hand in hand at last they drank together, united not only by the shared pleasure of Coca-Cola, but by a spirit of true universal brotherhood.

Coke
Trade-mark®
Catch the wave. Coke®

Coke is it!®
Coca-Cola
Coke
LOVE YA CAIPO
スカッとさわやか コカ・コーラ
Enjoy Coca-Cola
TRADE MARK REGD

In 1971 the famous "Hill Top" advertisement was simultaneously broadcast in all countries, achieving what young people aspired to — a world without frontiers. It showed young people in their national costumes, representing some 30 countries. Together in a group on a hillside, they sang the appealing jingle, "I'd like to buy the world a home, and furnish it with love, grow apple trees and honey bees and snow white turtle doves." And not for eight lines was Coca-Cola mentioned.

In the very first week the advertisement screened, more than 4000 letters of approval arrived in Atlanta from young people. The pop group, the New Seekers, were licensed to make a non-commercial version of the jingle. It reached the top of the hit parade and royalties were donated to UNICEF. The ad appealed to all ages and established once and for all Coca-Cola's universal charisma.

Poster made from stills of the famous 1971 "Hillside" commercial.

ETERNAL, IMMORTAL, SUPERSTAR

So, today, as we approach the 1990s, The Coca-Cola Company is uniquely placed, through its diverse business operations, to provide millions of people world-wide with refreshment and enjoyment from films, fruit juices and, of course, soft drinks — led by the seemingly eternal star, Coca-Cola.

Coca-Cola has a unique image as a symbol of things that are good, enjoyable and refreshing. Millions of people of all ages, creeds and colors, living in more than 150 countries, ask for it in 80 or more languages every day. Like the great film stars — Marilyn Monroe, James Dean, John Wayne — Coca-Cola has become an immortal, universal superstar in its own right. Drunk by the famous, by children in China, Arabs in the desert, cricketers in Australia and vacationers in Britain, "the pause that refreshes."

Who would have imagined that Coca-Cola and the Statue of Liberty, both first exposed to the public in 1886, would each in its own way become a universally recognized symbol of the American way of life?

What would the founder of it all, Dr. John Pemberton, think if he could see the giant enterprise now? To know what has grown from his original recipe and that his 1886 description of the drink, "Delicious and Refreshing," provided a theme and an image that would still be around more than a hundred years later, and with which people all round the world would identify; for whom today, "Coke is it" — the superstar.

Appendix:

THE WORDS THAT SAY IT

How many Coca-Cola slogans are there? Hundreds, of course, of which a chronological selection is given here.

Going through those used from 1886 to 1986 one sees that the message has had a consistent theme, emphasizing the thirst-quenching, pleasure-giving properties and social benefits of Coca-Cola. The continuing simplicity of the message has benefited the trademark by helping to make it unforgettable. A deeper analysis could identify the most frequently used words. Certainly "refresh," used right through from 1886, would have to take first place.

Slogan	Year
Delicious! Refreshing! Exilarating! Invigorating.	1886
Delightful summer and winter beverage.	1895
Deliciously refreshing.	1900
The most refreshing drink in the world.	1904
Delicious and refreshing.	1904
Wherever you go you'll find Coca-Cola.	1905
Cooling . . . refreshing . . . delicious.	1907
After the day's journey drink a glass of delicious, refreshing, Coca-Cola. It satisfies the thirst and pleases the palate. It relieves fatigue and imparts new vigor and new energy. Cooling. Refreshing.Delicious.	1909
Happy Days.	1910
It's time to drink Coca-Cola.	1911
A welcome addition to any party — any time —anyplace.	1913
The best beverage under the sun.	1913
A drink of all the year.	1917
Coca-Cola is a perfect answer to thirst that no imitation can satisfy.	1919
A natural drink that answers natural thirst.	1919
The answer to thirst.	1922
Thirst knows no season.	1922
Refresh yourself.	1923
Pause and refresh yourself.	1924
Everybody likes it.	1925

PAUSE
TRINK
Coca-Cola

Enjoy the sociable drink. 1925
Coca-Cola is the shortest distance between thirst and refreshment. 1926
Stop at the red sign. 1926
The pause that refreshes. 1929
The drink that makes the pause refreshing. 1932
It invites a pause. 1933
Refreshing as a morning dip. 1935
Coca-Cola . . . the pause that brings friends together. 1935

Haddon Sundblom's famous Santa Claus Coke advertisements: Above 1941; lower, 1938. Opposite: 1951.

. . . talk about being *good* !

Coca-Cola invites you to lunch.	1937
Stop for a pause . . . go refreshed.	1937
Any time is the right time to pause and refresh.	1938
Thirst asks nothing more.	1938
The drink everybody knows.	1939
Thirst stop here.	1939
Coca-Cola belongs.	1941
Everybody welcomes Coca-Cola—it's the real thing.	1942
Coca-Cola is good.	1943
Universal symbol of the American way of life.	1943
Pause — Go refreshed.	1944
Coca-Cola helps show the world the friendliness of American ways.	1945
That's for me.	1945
The friendliest club in the world.	1946
Yes.	1946
Relax with the pause that refreshes.	1947
Happy hour ... have a Coke.	1947
Think of lunchtime as refreshment time.	1948
Refresh - and add zest to the hour.	1950
Refreshment through the years.	1951

The 1954 slogan.

For home and hospitality.	1951
Good with so many things.	1951
The gift for thirst.	1952
What you want is a Coke.	1952
Coke time.	1954
Have a Coke and be happy.	1954
Young America loves it.	1954
The friendliest drink on earth.	1956
Taste the difference.	1956
Sign of good taste.	1957
Coke is just right.	1957

1954

1946

Refreshment the whole world prefers.	1958
Happy pause for the youth of all ages.	1958
Relax refreshed.	1959
Welcome as springtime.	1959
Coke refreshes you best.	1960
Relax with Coke.	1960
Only Coca-Cola refreshes you best.	1962
Lift that livens.	1962
Things go better with Coke.	1963
People go better refreshed.	1964
You'll go better refreshed.	1964
Enjoy Coca-Cola.	1965
This is the time for real refreshment.	1965
Coke . . . after Coke . . . after Coke.	1966
It's twice time.	1968
Tells your taste to go fly a kite.	1968
Go with Coke.	1969
Things go better with Coke — Coke is the real thing.	1970
Coke adds life . . .	1974-75

Have a Coke and a smile.	1978-79
Coke is it.	1982
We've got a taste for you. (Coca-Cola)	1985
America's real choice. (Coca-Cola Classic)	1985
Red, white & you. (Coca-Cola Classic)	1986
Catch the wave. (Coca-Cola)	1986
When Coca-Cola is part of your life, you can't beat the feeling.	1987

A variation of the 1952 slogan "What you want is a Coke."

Bevete
Coca-Cola
Coca-Cola
OM
Coca-Cola
Bevete
Coca-Cola
170

Coca-Cola
Coca-Cola
Coca-Cola
Coca-Cola

ENJOY

Coca-Cola
Coca-Cola
Coca-Cola
Coca-Cola

CENTENNIAL CELEBRATION

Illustration credits:
Visual Service (pp. 4, 81, 82-85, 86-87, 104-105, 107, 111 lower)
Photo Service — Gruppo Editoriale Fabbri (p. 55)
Grazia Neri/J. Andanson-Sygma (p. 50-51)
Fredi Marcarini (p.100)
All other illustrations: The Coca-Cola Company

6. Australia, 7. Austria 8. Bahamas 9. Barbados 10. Belgium

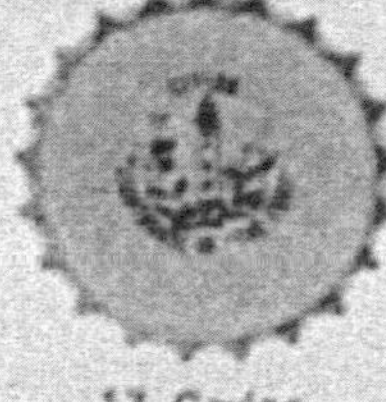

16. Canada 17. Ceylon 18. Chile 19. Colombia 20. Republic of the C

ominican Republic 27. Ecuador 28. Egypt 29. El Salvador 30. Ethiopi

36. Ghana 37. Gibraltar 38. Grenada 39. Guadeloupe 40. Guam

46. Iceland 47. India 48. Indonesia 49. Iran 50. Iraq

56. Kenya 57. Kuwait 58. Lebanon 59. Liberia 60. Malaga

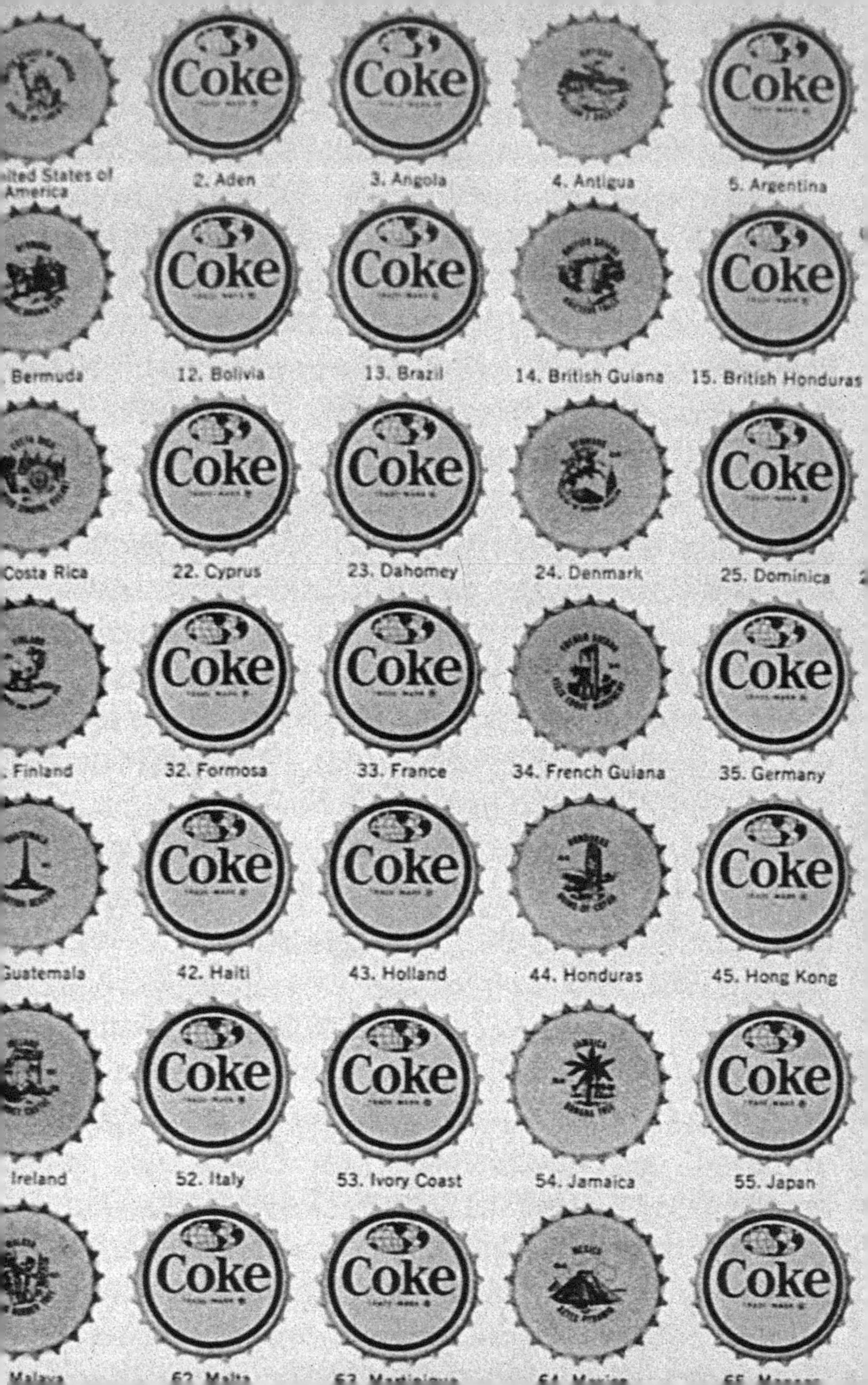
ited States of America
2. Aden
3. Angola
4. Antigua
5. Argentina
Bermuda
12. Bolivia
13. Brazil
14. British Guiana
15. British Honduras
Costa Rica
22. Cyprus
23. Dahomey
24. Denmark
25. Dominica
Finland
32. Formosa
33. France
34. French Guiana
35. Germany
Guatemala
42. Haiti
43. Holland
44. Honduras
45. Hong Kong
Ireland
52. Italy
53. Ivory Coast
54. Jamaica
55. Japan
Malaya
62. Malta
63. Martinique
64. Mexico
65. Macao